M000287289

Altadena Literary Review 2020

edited by

Teresa Mei Chuc & Hazel Clayton Harrison

Altadena Literary Review 2020

Copyright © 2020 by Shabda Press

Editor-in-Chief: Teresa Mei Chuc
Editor: Hazel Clayton Harrison

All rights reserved. No part of this book may be reproduced or transmitted in any form or by any means without written permission of the author.

Library of Congress Control Number: 2019912058

ISBN: 978-0-9600931-5-1

California native rose featured cover art & design by Kristen Torralba https://www.kt-art.com/

Published by Shabda Press
Pasadena, CA 91107
www.shabdapress.com

Contents

Prose...305

Acknowledgment

Thank you to Tovaangar, the ancestral land of the Tongva people, with her native plants and animals, which encompasses the Los Angeles Basin, on which we are guests, and thank you to the Tongva people.

Thank you to The Friends of the Altadena Library for funding the printing of the *Altadena Literary Review 2020* and the Poetry & Cookies release reading for the *ALR 2020*.

Thank you to the editorial committee for their hard work, dedication and keen eyes:
Carla Sameth, Pauli Dutton, Cathie Sandstrom, Mary Fitzpatrick, Khadija Anderson, Gerda Govine, Toni Laudermilk, Hazel Clayton Harrison (Editor), Teresa Mei Chuc (Editor-in-Chief)

Thank you to Thelma T. Reyna, Elline Lipkin and Pauli Dutton for your support, guidance and for paving the way.

Thank you to Victor Cass for suggesting the new title, Altadena Literary Review

Introduction

The voices in the Altadena Literary Review 2020 are diverse and beautiful as the flora and fauna of Tovaangar, the ancestral land of the Tongva people, which includes Los Angeles. The poetry and prose of the people we see every day who also carry poems within their hearts...from people experiencing houselessness to the youth to your neighbor. We are grateful to bring voices of poets/writers in this book writing words, in addition to English, in the Tongva language, Nahuatl language, Spanish, Vietnamese, and Chinese. Within this diversity is the song of life, death, suffering, hope and joy reminding us how connected we are to each other and life on this planet and the universe.

Teresa Mei Chuc, Editor-in-Chief
Altadena Poet Laureate 2018 to 2020
Altadena Literary Review 2020

When Teresa and I started our journey as co-Altadena poets laureate in 2018, we had no idea of the opportunities and challenges our new titles would bring. Since then we have grown tremendously as poets, publishers and champions for the literary arts.

The *Altadena Literary Review 2020* represents the culmination of two years of our efforts to promote poetry and letters, and serves as a historical record of our vision to publish a literary journal that upholds excellence and reflects the diverse voices of not only the Altadena and Pasadena communities, but of greater Los Angeles. Thus, within these pages you will hear a chorus of multi-ethnic voices, as well as voices that represent members of the LGBTQ communities and different socio-economic groups, from those living in million dollar manors to those living in tents. You will hear their love songs and laments, their ditties, dirges, and dreams. By listening we hope you will not only develop a better understanding of the human condition, but a greater empathy and compassion for all of humankind.

Hazel Clayton Harrison, Editor
Altadena Poet Laureate 2018—2020
Altadena Literary Review 2020

On Loving

I.

In the verdugo woodlands, I saw a falcon

make his slow descent upon what I mistook
for a gardenia. One animal sinking

claws into another like a bouquet of red
and white. I thought of how folklore interprets

the owl as a good omen, except for Arabs,
who believe the raptor to hold the soul

of a tormented man. How verdugo can mean
switch or whip or tyrant.

II.

I've loved within an inch of my life,
fists tied. But I keep thinking

how you held my hands last night
turning them over and inspecting

them like coins. The softest,
you said. I wanted you to lift one

to your face, to contemplate the knuckles,
brush them against your lips, like I did
with my mother's as a child. I wanted to feel
your prickle. But I have learned to be

quiet as prey. What you don't know
is that I could moan

into the mouth of the devil himself.
I could forgive.

And what about that demon who peddled
my heart? In another life he's sawing off

these same fingers that can coax the sheen
of hair on your arm to stand upright.

III.

He wants to believe himself
a martyr. He wants to be the crushing

orange light of dusk. He wants to be the lone
kestrel that descends upon the field.

What you don't know is
I have lured such vultures. I have watched

a hawk take the soft petals of a dove
into its mouth, and without flinching,

I asked, what is that beautiful bird?
Can it love me?

by Jessica Abughattas

*Published: *The Journal* (Ohio State University) September 2018

Animal Feeling

I wanted to wake with you and the cat
in a small house at the foot of a mountain

where birds sing wildly into the dusk
and coyotes scavenge from yard to yard

stalking timid dogs and fat neighborhood cats,
but not ours. Ours tiptoes in at the first ray

and climbs over us – a gymnast, sweet boy.
You must be there now. The cottage

between Hen's Tooth Plaza and the hiking trail
that leads to an abandoned train station.

They must stay doing that even without me.
Of course they do: the birds proclaiming nothing,

the cats yawning from their roofs
and drainpipes, the lawns humming

wet with dew, the plaza sitting vacant
awaiting the keys of laborers, the rattlesnakes

hissing on the trail, early sun just hitting
their skin, the tracks collecting dust

and staring out into the city below,
where I have gone. I wake alone

in a room on the boulevard: cars
are rushing to offices, tires screeching

as they go, and people waiting on the sidewalks
for a ride, or their dog to piss.

It all keeps going on without you.
The little flame in the sky, it just has to

go and touch us all.

by Jessica Abughattas

Second Hand

Los Alamos, California

Alma, eighty, makes me a deal: the vintage mink, silk gown,
cherry-printed handkerchiefs. She names her price, unfurls

the frock, says I'm the only slip of a girl to pass through town
the thing actually fits. It's a finger-on-the-trigger place

midway up the western coast, where truckers try
their hands at dainty waitresses, or a choir girl with a waist

like Farrah Fawcett—the apple of her mother's black eye.
In a Victorian mansion converted to an antique shop

a Victrola turns like a lover's worry. The owner's daughters
follow me around. Porcelain dolls, age five and seven. They know

where the prettiest dresses hang. I wear my winnings, trying
on another life in a bathroom with a dusty tub and a door

that won't shut, skipping home in the dark to a man, asleep
in my motel room: his beautiful drooling face. His body

an orchard, heavy on the bed with dumb love. What luck.
I want to say: I bet so many girls have loved you. Have you

grown tired yet of admiration? Have you even dreamed of dying
some Chris McCandless death, in the lonesome landscape

of the mind? But I don't say anything. I just dance around
in a thrift store dress and no bra—basking in my accidental

inheritance. I know it's mine, and I'm here to take it back.

by Jessica Abughattas

*Earlier version published: *Heavy Feather Review,* June 2017

Thoughts from a Far Away Town

No one to my left. No one to my right. Just me and the wind and the falling snow in the purple orange of the morning. You would think I'm lost, but I'm not. I know this place all too well. I feel the aching in my bones and know it's winter. I feel tingling on my skin and know the sun will show up soon. I like these dark hours to myself while everyone else is sleeping. I can feel the rumbling of the town as it breathes and sighs in the dark. Morning will come soon, and this magic time will pass bringing different weather and colors. Morning will bring spring, midway will bring summer, evening will bring autumn, and night…winter. So fast the cycles turn, but so easy we have adapted. Not many others feel the same about winter as I do. Most keep their windows shut, curtains closed at night. But I welcome the cold and the silence. I welcome the dark sky, the static white air, the end of a cycle. The horizon filled with change.

by Micaela Accardi-Krown

Mexican of America

A Sonnet

Mestizo come, America, you call.
Amniotic oceans Pacific join,
break through the virgin hymen, wailing wall
from the fluids of her earthen loins.

Tender eyes burn with the new day's fire.
Bullets shatter your bones, your flesh torn on
border fences, electrified barbed wire.
Knives slash and puncture the sight of the dawn.

You are spewed out, volcanic bloodied birth.
Darkest rupture imploded then screamed out,
erupted from moist entrails of madre earth.
Wails of the heart burst purple veined brow.

Desire from the depths, takes new day's flight.
America with stars of shattered light.

by Vibiana Aparicio-Chamberlin

What I Know

I know this much--that you know and understand what is sacred and should not be disturbed because you say "You can not move the Titanic...don't disturb those that are in their watery grave."

Don't disturb their graves...

I also know this much--that you know and understand what hallowed ground is Because you say "Where the Twin Towers once stood is hallowed ground...it must be re-spected."

Don't build or develop on that ground...

Why is it you lack understanding, compassion and respect for our ancestral burial grounds, being decimated, desecrated, in the name of home building as the developer proclaims I have all the correct paperwork, blue prints and permissions,
get the hell out of our way,
we have a time schedule
keep the back hoes digging
those are not human remains
these damn trouble makers
I am loosing money...

The politicians agree...they try to cover up...

Then a halt and the salivating anthropologists are sent in with their students to remove what was sent into the spirit world in ceremony with burial items for their next journey…so very sacred

   We must study these items
     categorize,
       catalog
         define
           store them in boxes
              put them in dusky warehouses
                the academic world must study
                  perhaps we will let them
                              bury them some day

Those who will not give up remain in a prayer vigil for the ancestors.

I know and understand this…don't disturb the burials…leave them undisturbed
You must understand this

by Gloria Arellanes

"What I Know" first appeared in *News from Native California* magazine

Staging Purple

Crocus crescendos
From the orchestra pit

Wisteria waits in the wings
Her descending arms ready to blossom

She wistfully wanders
Into the scene
Dancing delicately
Wafting her sensuous scent

Catnip chorus
Sways to the lilt of the tune
Lowly lit
Perfectly positioned
Near the upstage backdrop

Salvia Indigo's surprise arrival
Satiates the audience's desire
Standing up for encores

Spring's run will be
Glorious
The critics note

by Beth Baird

The Wave

I rise from sitting
I stand to face the approaching menace
The soothing, rhythmic pounding of breakers on the shore
No longer

Staring at my nemesis
Unable to move
All body functions freeze
I succumb to its force field

Scientists explain the reason for this turn of events
Chemicals triggered in the brain
Cataclysmic circumstances climax

Praying I will surface from the blackness
As the tsunami wave of depression
Hits my shore

by Beth Baird

Appeared previously in *On Sunday the Danube Flows*, Poetry of participants of 55th Belgrade International Writers' Meetings / Editor Milan Pani, Belgrade Writer's Association of Serbia, 2018.

Planting Seeds in Hope of Planting Herself

Every fruit is an experiment to her
Will it grow if she soaks the seed?
Jars adorn the windowsills
With avocado and mango seeds
Lovingly pierced with toothpicks
Sitting in embryonic water
Awaiting a shoot   a root   to plant

Transplanting herself to Los Angeles
Fearing nothing will grow for her here
The soil is tired
Arid climate produces a 10% chance
Of rain
Of new friends

The odds not in her favor
She brings seedlings home
Plants them lovingly in bigger pots
Time and rain will prove
Her success or not

Wait.........

Spying yellow flowers on tomato plants
Hope springs from the stem!
From her efforts
From her care
From her love

by Beth Baird

The Cloud Rider

On a wisp of cloud he rides,
in white top hat & tails.
Small in stature,
straight and proud,
an ebony baton in hand,
with arms outstretched he
silently calls to the heavens
and at once the winds come
from every direction.

Solid and strong,
he stands ready to begin.
He waves the black baton
in a flourish of infinity
and in so doing, conjoins and
commingles the winds,
the north with the south, east,
and west, strong and weak.

In that moment of shift
there comes a harmonious hum
as with hands and heart
the Cloud Rider conducts
the winds in a sweet
seductive symphony
and together they sing
joyfully to the Earth

When the people of Earth hear,
they lay down their arms,
and abandon their greed,
hate and fear, as the mighty
winds sing gloriously
united as one.

Satisfied, the Cloud Rider
lowers the black baton,
bows his head and is once
more a smiling, senile
old man in a wheel-chair.

by Judy Barrat

Semper Virens

A woman is always considered
An unfinished work.

A man often reaches
His full height
And never reaches again.

The woman trees keep growing
And the man trees wither.

Where is the tree
That will entwine its branches
With that of another tree,
Its rightful mate?

If we go on growing
And they don't
We are left alone.

Men, spread out your arms.
Let the leaves grow.
Let the branches harden.
Let the work go on
And the work be in progress.
For how else
Can we re-leaf the world?

by Lynn Bronstein

Sonnet of the Homme Fatale

Danger always gave me his kiss
of nicotine dread. I kept his house warm

job after job. Back he'd come and five shots
later he's out by design. Did I deserve this?

Morning sirens drew him to the windows,

the doorbell drew him to his gun,

but today I'll rub his neck and pour my fugitive

something slow, to give the law some time.

Every man has said to me "we got it made"
the minute before a gunshot.
I could never turn from his deadly kisses
but now I put my tongue to use anew.

Fate, he mumbled, getting cuffed, first name John.

One final pinch, my love, from me to you.

by Jeffrey Bryant

Ho Chi Minh Meanders

His black pajamas creaseless
and slung across his protruding
collarbones
Brow slightly singed with sweat
Uncle Ho leisurely strolls
along Garden Grove with clasped
hands behind his back
He makes a sucking sound between
his teeth
savouring a bitter after-dessert taste
Growing sleepy at the sight of
palm trees violently sloughing
last year's wildfire ash
The patriots sing foreign songs
now and wear deader eyes
than the long dead
Uncle Ho wipes his nose
with his sleeve
and lets the residue dry

How can victory be so
grotesque? Like fish
over-salted, he balks
while he walks

The slap of his sandals
like helicopter thwaps

beat
beat
beating sickly retreat.

by Tommy Vinh Bui

A Gift

Though not the first to speak these words, I still
will say, though far too short, this life is yet
a wondrous gift. The challenge is to fill
our days with joy until our sun has set.

Each breath I draw might then my soul awake.
Each light that strikes my eye may then reveal
such worlds afloat in golden motes as make
far worlds unknown, unseen, seem real.

And now upon a narrow trail I tread
above the plunging canyons wild and steep;
and in the west the sun is brightly spread
upon the mighty ocean broad and deep.

And I alone, in splendor bright immersed,
am, by the light, in love of life well versed.

by Tim Callahan

Also My Heart

a ghazal

If I could cure mind and soul from the ravages of rogues – and also my heart,
my mind and body would be whole, and so, also my heart.

The officious and petty ensnare me in a rigmarole set to frustrate my visions.
For they would, if they could, control my thoughts and also my heart.

Who knows what online post hides a troll full of malice and venom,
who, in this most perverse role, would kill my passions, also my heart?

Who knows what those scoundrels stole, who have burdened
my emotions and mind and made their goal also my heart?

Despite designs of villains, black as coal, friends throng about me
to salve their vile vitriol, to save my reason and also my heart.

Poetry foils the abuses louts dole out with such hatred.
It strengthens my will and helps console also my heart.

One love, across a treacherous shoal, steers me in an irregular
course to cajole me to create with my joys and fears, and also my heart.

Rising from the darkest, most tropic hole, undeterred by evil plots and schemes,
I ascend to a chill and shining pole that refreshes my spirit and also my heart.

by Tim Callahan

Fairy Duster

With such a name for such a plant
you'd think it's something delicate.
And so it seems as so it spreads
its fine and ferny feathery leaves.
and raises bright and brushy
ethereal flowers flaming red.

And with whirring thrumming
drumming wings the hummingbirds
are hovering standing in the air.
With hair-like tongues they taste
the nectar of the blazing blooms
so fine and fair, adding their fragility
to the shrub's exquisite symmetry.

And yet the duster rises up most
elegant above the grim gray dirt
so dry and harsh in the heartless heat.
And still it rises flaming fair and
green and graceful, seeming
tender in the drought. It is a desert
plant of iron will and steely strength.

by Tim Callahan

Fireworks

a street tree
exploding with magenta
flowers, each like a fourth
of July fireball in August
spiraling out of the green
held up by brown trunk
on the smooth grass
of a traffic meridian
--and look--there's
another one on
a different island
and again, over here
boom boom boom
bloom bloom bloom

by Don Kingfisher Campbell

Cross Town Muse

You came to me while I was riding the bus
Driving me to write then and there
But I didn't know how to begin
You opened the door
Every jarring movement
Compelled new words
Opened spaces
Closed doubts
Introduced me to my heroine
Down Wilshire we flew
She had red hair
A riveting stare
Her energy pushed me through corridor after corridor
I couldn't write the words down fast enough
Crossing Fairfax
Vermont
At Westmoreland she taxed me with her fervor
Pushing me on building a fire storm
Crossing Figueroa
Then Flower
Alameda train tracks
Don't be afraid to stumble
One wild horse to another.

by Christine Candland

mountain lilac

you take me back
to a hike I made
surrounded by women
but mostly alone
we walked through the
fog covered chaparral

not desperate stars burning
through a soulless night
terrifying and illuminating
imploding into black holes
or crashing through emptiness

just myself
and a dozen women
walking silently through the fog
surrounded by purple and white blossoms
of mountain lilac and an aching
emptiness for what we left behind

by Peggy Castro

Bamboo Patio

I wear marigold vestidas from Mazatlán
and a necklace bedazzled in topaz stone,
bestowed upon my neckline by Aunt Violeta
from her septiembre cruise to Puerto Vallarta.

My favorite kind of drink
is Tamarindo
on a glass top table in our bamboo patio
I hear our parrot Zephyr babble to the breeze
and neighborhood Chihuahuas

behind manzanita leaves.
Chain link divides their snarls from me,
crows trapeze sunlight in our in-between alley.
I sit before my easel,
watercolor the city.

by Chuka Susan Chesney

Muzak / Music

What's exactly
The difference between
Muzak and Music but

The difference in the
Pronunciation of
"myoozak" vs. "myoozik" - which

Is exactly
The difference of two sound bites
Which happens to

Signify
All of
The differences

Between the signifier
and
The signified

Between the evasive Form
and
The elusive Content

Between what is spoken
and what is
Unspeakable

As in a poem

In all poems
In poetry

As in a lyric, set to a melody
Sang from the depth of the heart, where
Instruments become instrumental
Like poetry
Like music

by Philip Chiao

Chinese Zither (Zheng)

One time, overhearing
a wisecrack I made
You handed me
a piece of single folded paper containing
a few lines you wrote
I reciprocated with
a poem of my own
Copied in my best Chinese handwriting onto
an 8-1/2x11 sheet of gridded paper
Folded in trifold and inserted into
a letter sized envelope
I stopped by your dorm, but you were out
I slid the envelope under your door

It has been said that Chinese poetry has
a range of sounds like Zheng, heavy as storms
Hitting the ridge of mountains, light as pearls
Dropping into jade vessels

But by now I no longer possess
either storms or pearls, I have
Lost my steam, ever so
gently, innocently until
My mind awakens to
a linguistic junk yard of
Broken Chinese characters, twisted sounds and
Shredded images, indeed I have
Lost my marbles and

Can no longer play
"The Glass Bead Game"

We met again at the thirty year college reunion
We chatted around topics at cocktail hours
During dinner
We sat at different tables
Then you walked over, tapped me on the shoulder, and
Left me with
a quarter folded cocktail napkin
The single square unfolded into four squares to reveal
a Chinese poem you just wrote
My hand trembled as I folded it back and
Tucked it into my vest

I did not say

a single word
I knew the only sensible thing to do was to return
Your poem with
a poem

I have attempted to write again
I have chosen to write in
a second language that
I now claim as my own
Should I or could I play
a violin as if it were
a Zheng?
Or let violin be violin?

I do not know how you might react
I am not sure if
I will send my poems to you —
fifteen years has passed since

by Philip Chiao

Why I Write

I write. Miles and miles of magnetic words, draw your world to mine, in our shared galaxy. Words that can halt time, capture your face, preserved in notebooks, no matter where you are.

your face
absent from photographs
the wrinkles you hid
now etched onto the page
in the shapes of words

by Jackie Chou

--Previously published in Atlas Poetica 38, 2019

Mother of Water, River of Nine Dragons

"Dam construction on the Mekong River poses a serious threat to the region's economies and ecosystems. The only way to mitigate that threat is to end defiant unilateralism and embrace institutionalized collaboration focused on protecting each country's rights and enforcing its obligations – to its people, its neighbors, and the planet." – Brahma Chellaney (August 2, 2019)

Sông Mê Kông, flowing from the Tibetan Plateau
through China, Myanmar,
Laos, Thailand, Cambodia, Vietnam
and into the country of my heart

where the wild rice grows
and the villagers live and have lived
for thousands of years,

where the Irrawaddy dolphins,
the giant catfish and the softshell turtles swim,

where the sarus cranes feed
on insects, seeds, fish in the river reeds,
and open their majestic wings to take flight,

where the lilies and lotus bloom,
where our ancestors are alive,

where the water buffalo bathe
their thousand-pound body
submerged in the river of my soul
their heads on the water's surface
curving horns pointing towards the sky,

where Sông Cửu Long,
River of Nine Dragons flow
through thick palm and green mangrove forests
where the douc langur and white-cheeked gibbon exist,

and the salt and fresh water mix,

I, your daughter, am forever connected to you
though thousands of miles away.

by Teresa Mei Chuc

"Mother of Water, River of Nine Dragons" was first published in *The Tiger Moth Review*, Issue 3

He Was My Church

I could go whenever I wanted
to the back room at Jones Coffee- the secret space,
Clarke was my church
I stopped going on Sundays

There our knees bumped together on the black plastic settee.
Clarke's endless legs bent, his knees flying buttresses poking into the quiet.
We sipped sacramental cappuccino while Clarke's long fingers
broke his roll into crumbles on it's way to his mouth.
Flakes from a perfect croissant scattered on his sweater, the seat, the floor
sprinkled holy. This is my body.
We filled up our own goodness with each other.
We shared books – the ones that changed our lives.
We shared movies.
We both knew we were Zorba when we watched
Anthony Quinn dancing in the sand.

Clarke always spread his passion outward
We even went Greek dancing in a
Scandinavian Hall in Pasadena
then he arranged to have the Quinn movie shown at his luxe facility.
We watched it in the screening room with the old folks.
One of the residents slid out of her seat right onto the floor.
We are old but we would never be that old.

Clarke read books peeking beyond death where he planned to go any minute
to be reunited with Wendy, his beloved wife.
Proof of Heaven, and *Love Beyond Death*, were big.
To bridge the gap Clarke and I went to seances together.

Clarke did not wait for the crystal glass to choose him, He commanded his wife.

His fingers in the air above the little oval table, he touched her, you could see it.

You could here her in his voice.

He told her, "Be patient, I'll be with you soon enough. She said not to worry, "I am with you all the time. Did you know who jostles you at night when you get into a funny position?"

Wendy and Clarke don't need the crystal glass anymore.

I do. I hope he jostles me when I get stuck.

by Marsha Cifarelli

long shadows drape over
living things effortlessly

The air gets crisp with melted grass
on quiet, hot days in Southern California.
The sidewalk makes its move to dehydrate
back to cement powder.

Crows and Lantana
glide their skeletons at the sun.
Peeling dashboard covers under its boot.
Even the basement is hot with the sun.

Lantana glows easily
towards it,
as if the sun were a
cool, moss-edged pool.

Crows glare back at the glare
to measure the cat's eye
against other marbles,
buttons and round shiny things.

Crow collects, sorts
and radiates it onto the lawn,
like a grandparent's knitting pattern.

You don't have to look at it.
Your arms dangle like hot seatbelts.
Your skin wrinkles more rapidly.

Skeins on the lawn
connecting one corner
of skin to the other.

Cool sheets over hot skin,
cover old furniture.

The sidewalk is cracked where
a tree used to stand.

You wouldn't know it if you hadn't seen it.

by Reg Clarkinia   *female*

Grey Matter

Sometimes I feel trapped
within myself

I can see out but
no one else can see in

I am a rotating kaleidoscope
a whirling pinwheel

I am up and down,
sideways and slanting

I am dripping off a cliff
of moral enlightenment

...

Where does the light
come from

How do I speak to it
and ask it to stay

Why is there only darkness
that surrounds me
Why is the real answer

always grey
I want to live in
technicolor moments

Freeze frame happiness
and keep it in clear view

...

but no one can hear
me

My screams are softer than
silkworms spinning kisses

I am draped and covered in
molded moss

At the bottom of
a swamp

How do you love what you
scrape off of your shoes

by Coco

Harvest Season

They know not of this land
How it came to be and what makes it grand

To reap and to sow
To plow and to mow

The grain grown through grit and through pain
How laborers died in the heat and in the rain

THE HARVEST HAS COME
Praise shouts across the land

But do you know the bountiful harvest
Grown by each woman and man

By children just learning to walk
No time for loose lips that now begin to talk

No time to play
These seeds must be sown by the end of the day

Tell me again to whom you give thanks
Did you come to discover their bellowing angst

Which crop filled your bowl to the brim
While others go hungry their outlook so grim

Feast and be merry
No need to be weary

For the Harvest Season has come

by Coco

Immigration Status: Grieving

Immigration
Complex red-tape entanglement
Humanity lost in the dossier
Documents of birth,
filled applications, and fees
Pero sin papeles para el luto

Without the therapy of a funeral
No six-feet deep burials
Dressed in black
Next to a casket
Mourning the painful fact
of forever gone.

Grieving death in the distance
The dead still live in the soul
In the mind
Never tangible
Never finite
No visas for grieving.

by Lisbeth Coiman

A Protective Shroud

Last night
During my brief slumber
I crocheted a protective cloak for you to take on your journey

At the airport,
As I said my goodbyes
I placed the shawl on your shoulders
To keep you warm
To shield you
from the ravaging storm

I remain here
Praying through this poem
No devotions, no gods or *hailmaries*
I only had these words as offering
for you to come back to me

In the dream I told you,
Go home, dear friend/husband
To your mother
To our homeland
To the war against the tyrant
On your lips, my kisses.
On your shoulders, my tears.

While I remained here
Holding onto what we used to be.

by Lisbeth Coiman

Second Law of Newton

To my parents on my 55th birthday

Twenty-year therapy
Learning the laws of letting go
Excavating / medicating
Trauma
Thinking forgiveness inhabits a kingdom
For which I bear no passport or entry visa
While holding the past
With both hands folded over chest
A survival trophy

Until reality feels like dystopia
Until your brief voice message
Says, "Your father weighs 112 pounds."
Or brother's WhatsApp reads
"I was able to bring them water today.
They've had no electricity for a week."

Till no solid ground
Exerting a force equal to
The weight of my resentment on your shoulders
Can hold your feeble legs
In the line for a monthly ration.

To extend my hands to you
I surrender
Let go.

by Lisbeth Coiman

Daisies are Pinwheeling

Daisies are pinwheeling, pinwheeling, pinwheeling,

streaking the sky in a sunshine processional,
praising in noonhymning tunes, seedbright ditties

and petalwhite prophecies, chanting their cheerful
irrelevancies over greengrowing earth,

and behold all the seawaving grasses' susurrus
of sunflooded ripples, their barleygold glowing

in low ululations of earthy responses
and slow jubilations below, swaying, piedpiped

by pinwheeling daisies! Of what do they dream,
to what springsummer humming crescendos, what babble

of brightening images flung among meadowdawn
winds, do they dance, and what ambercrammed panpipes

enrapt them when daisies go pinwheeling over them,
streaking the sky, and all over us daisies

are pinwheeling, pinwheeling, pinwheeling, pinwheeling?

by Stephen Colley

Opening a Chrysalis

What if our time on earth is not the main event?
What if its trials are merely practice for unimpeded
flight?

Like the caterpillar,
whose existence is to survive the perils of earthbound life
while assimilating everything in its path
then, hibernate in a self made sleeping bag
long enough to grow wings.

My beloved friend, Laura, is such a creature
having lived a life full of adventure and magic
touching all who came into her sphere with
grace and humor creating a ripple that will
continue long after she has taken flight.

Those of us who have known her and been
forever changed are watching now as she prepares
for takeoff into the next dimension.
Her once vital form danced and hiked and mentored
us all, talking with her hands, taking delight in small
expressions of beauty as she taught us to make
the most of each day and stretch a birthday celebration
into a month or more. We watched as she masterfully
spun a web of social connections wherever she went
that became the matrix of her support now.

The once fiercely independent trailblazer must now
accept assistance and is somehow able to shift
with grace, humility and gratitude.

I associate the monarch butterfly with her vibrant
spirit. When I saw one peering in my windows
and drinking nectar from my flowers I just knew it was
Laura's spirit taking a test flight before her wings are fully
formed, visiting me in a space she has never been, and
in so doing reassuring me that her next adventure is
forthcoming
and the flight plan approved.

by Chris Cressey

My Mother's Father

My grandfather's heart
pumped peppermint Schnapps
through icy veins

My grandfather's lungs
bestowed a home to
too many Camels

My grandfather's fingers
shortened years before
caressed only the back of his dog

My grandfather's voice
machine-gunned in
volume and speed

My grandfather's sperm
fathered fourteen children
only three grown

My grandfather's brain
stewed a soup of
imagined wrongs

My grandfather scared me
One sister thought he was funny

by Pat Cross

The Uncles

The places they would gather
a confidence of men
with voices of grit and malt

At the kitchen table cards would fly
the deck stripped down the black queen ruled
Faces so clearly drawn from the same pool
I struggled each meeting to recall who was who

In our back yard on a summer Sunday
seated in Adirondack chairs built by their brother
they passed the bucket of beer hand to hand
told stories not meant for little girls' ears

Musicians, poets, artists
masquerading as
street sweepers, postmen, brewery workers
they lived in a golden age
with callused hands and joyful hearts

by Pat Cross

Tears for Tosca on a Saturday Afternoon

In a flat on the lower east side of Milwaukee
antimacassars grace the brushed burgundy
sofa and chair

Sun shines through the lace curtains
to dot the African violets
placed just so on the round table

The radio console stands
against the dusty rose wall
an amber glow across its dial

We are tuned to the Met
and as the notes float out
and drift across the room
to settle in my father's ear

tears flow quietly down his cheeks.

by Pat Cross

Dispatches

In the end, if she
was not oblivious, my
mother's saboteur
steeped her in dementia
making death more like a cure.

Dad hugged me at ten
when his mother died; then years,
my ire, and our pride
split us so that his passing
deterred us from another.

by Bill Cushing

Drydocks and Parades

The warm breezes of great heights
ran through fine
light hair
as I straddled
my father's neck,
gripping tight to his collar
as veterans marched proudly by:
Ike's years then.

Days of wonderful dizziness,
looking at
that parade of men below me:

a fearful pleasure—like now,
climbing kingposts
and stanchions
of eighty-thousand ton tankers
built with half-inch steel
and starplate from the keel up —
using cables, rivets, bolts,
torches, and welds.

by Bill Cushing

First published by *Undertow Tanka Review*, Jan. 2017

If The Sky Split Tonight

If the sky split tonight,
Dense seams peeled back
Stars flaking off, falling in
Drapes upon our shoulders
It would be from the crack
Our prayers made
Beat beat beating against the sky
Starting all those years ago
When ancestors
Lost,
Searched,
Struggled
To build themselves up again
In fields swaying with songs of endurance
Now echoing in the wind as
Heaven leaks out
To maybe soothe the earth
Or at least to give life to
Valves of recycled dreams
Passed down from generation to generation
A shell of our mother's mother's daydreams.
When I was a child I wanted—
Not even just as a child
I was—
Even now I—
Might have been a writer
She and grandpa wrote letters
When she was just 16 and he 18
And now at 76 and he, arching down from heaven,

Fingertips skimming through her dreams
She says
I've lived here, I've loved here, I'll die here!
Like the end of a play
Bowing to soaring roses
People rising, sitting, staring
With jewels in their eyes
And faces sloped like rain
Now ruptured with sun
Yes, Saginaw is her stage, but she never knew it
Gave birth and left her visions in the placenta
For her children to feed on
To say to her daughter
I always knew you'd be the one to do the things I couldn't
To sing along with Bessie Griffin
Sometimes I feel like I'm almost gone
To stare out windows
When I was a child I wanted—
not even just as a child
I was—
Even then I'd—
Work long night shifts
And remember Jim Crow
From middle school in South Carolina
Like it was yesterday
And so if you were to die having known her
She wouldn't take the train to bury you
And wouldn't take the train to see you if you were alive
And will instead plant trees for her grandchildren
Her neck strained low
Aching at the thought of you,
Praying that the weather where you are

Are the tears she cries for you here.

If the sky split tonight
Dense seams peeled back,
Stars
   Flaking
       Off
         Falling in
           Drapes
             Upon
               Her
                 Shoulders
                    She'd crack

A smile and breathe in her lover
As he welcomed her home.

by Triniti Daniel-Robinson

The Commute

I'd like to leap from these four wheels
So fast you'd hear the voices from the radio
Smear against each other
Their news liked blurred landscapes
Of jagged hills I'd throw myself against
Strewn limbs will stem like wildflowers
Scraping the dirt with their bowed heads
Praying to be rootless and to decorate the wind
Or maybe as offerings to people not yet ghosts
Or as a garnish on a grave, supple then brittle
Like the turn of night to day
When the sun enfolds night's cavern of stars
And makes blank skies hard to look at
Even now with dawn spreading
It is bruised and violent with birds calling each other to safety
And barren trees contorted like figures fruitlessly
Reaching for the hues of a sunrise
While silhouettes shuffle on sidewalks
Their walk drenched with
visionaries adopted as a child
And faceless angels
clinging to beings
demanding reality.

by Triniti Daniel-Robinson

Things Never Said

I go to high places to think of her
To wonder if in dim lit rooms she
Waded through the darkness in search of me
Or if it was just me squinting in the blue around us
stumbling back into edges where
Day's light cut into beautiful pieces of souvenir
As her words gleam like cherished jewels, I wished to carry.

I fell into you like lush summer grass
birds diving deeply in the sky
shrinking like the gnats flitting across the yard
I wanted to stare at the brown of your eyes,
wind curled in my hand like your fingers might,
and feel my heart lace with sun.

But instead I cradle your eyes across three-hour differences
With dreams still clinging to my mind
It's veiled fingers
Pointing out stars as if you are beside me
As the moon's blanched stare
softens my mind into
dense sand
filling out the hollowness of my bones
I am heavy and full enough now for immobility
But still stagger under dim lit streetlights
Following a mirage that claims your face

by Triniti Daniel-Robinson

Dusk

Lean into loss
like the dark
presses into the day—
Feel the way
she moves,
forms your grip,
chills your blood—
Watch the light retreat
like a child runs home—

And let her go.

by Stacy DeGroot

The Last Leaf

Forty feet up, the view from my office window
Reveals a tall, almost barren sycamore tree,
Trimmed with dry pods and a few muted red leaves.
Some leaves bob and nod as the winter winds blow.
Others are tossed about like rag dolls in the jaws of a Jack Russell.
My favorite, Eric, spins around in a circle
Like a pinwheel in gusty high winds.
Tenacious leaves, they, managing to hang on,
Clinging to life even as the tree,
In a schizophrenic phase,
Sends out tiny green shoots with the promise of spring.
What determines which leaf is the last to go?
Are all leaves equal, but some more equal than others?
When the last leaf falls, it will join its siblings on the lawn below.
When the last leaf begins its descent from forty feet,
Will it call out, "I won! I won!"?

by Valena Dismukes

previously published, *Eclectic Letters*, 2010

Mother Tongue[1]

My dominant language is English.
But who is to say if it is my primary language
When my family language is Cantonese?
I wonder what language
First fell from my lips
No -
First formed my thoughts
No -
First filled my ears
As I lay in my womb
Or is it my mother's womb,
Since it is my mother's body.
My mother...

My mother's tongue
Bends air into five different languages,
Tracing the history of the migration of her family
English
Cantonese
Vietnamese
Mandarin
Teo-Chow.
My mother's mother tongue is Teo-Chow.

I?
I don't know,
But I do feel,
I feel a mess of lack-of-rootedness
Without my mother('s) tongue.

by Tiffany Do

---

[1] Amy Tan

Thoughts from Underneath a Sunflower Leaf

I wanted to write a poem about big leaves,
And the view from underneath them,
And then I thought of how I don't hear those words often -
The view from the bottom.
It's more commonly
the view from up top,
the view from up here,
the view from above,
I wonder about the view from the bottom
The bottom of the food chain,
The bottom of society,
The bottom of my drink,
What is the view from rock bottom?
It's generally described as - not great.
It feels like a shitty place,
But how shitty?
Because in hitting rock bottom
Where there is no view,
Just dark blank emptiness
And I don't even know
How low I am
The question is not whether or not it's shit
It's about the quantity of shit -
How much shittiness is this really?
What the fuck is this shit?
Why the shit?
Where is this shit coming from?
Whose shit is this really?
Cause speaking of shits

Shit ain't so bad
Shit is great
Some shits make the best fertilizers
Worm poop, cow poop, in general,
Herbivore poops,
I'll throw in my exes too,
I composted all their rotten poop,
And with all this fertilizer,
This shit becomes delicious soil.
Soil for food
for nourishment
for the Land.
I think I want to be soil
Looking up at the undersides of big heart-shaped leaves.

by Tiffany Do

Intersection

The last time I tasted joy,
I walked along Crystal Cove,[2]
stretching my thoughts in sandy strides,
indulging the sun's caress
as my ankles kissed the changing tides

the last time I touched love,
celebrating with my wife and son,
laughter the grace over a savored meal,
falling into the moment's serenity,
hungrily inhaling all that I could feel

the last time I embraced hope,
I stood at the edge of the world,
the South African sunset at Cape Agulhas,[3]
strangers sharing rogue waves in wonder
that peace could roar like whispering thunder

by Mel Donalson

---

[2] A California state beach and park north of Laguna Beach
[3] The southern tip of South Africa where the Atlantic and Indian Oceans meet

Beasts

(for 8-year-old Asifa Bano, killed in
Kathua, India, in January 2018)

It wasn't your fault,
their madness is a disease as ancient
as the sickness it brings,
the beasts caught you in
that moment when angels stepped away,
your prayers unheard, your screams muffled
by the darkness in their merciless minds

your screams echoed to a wounded world,
one that begs your forgiveness,
that pleads for your understanding
that humankind is blind to those
who are precious like you,
who reminds us of what we might be
if we found courage to face the hostility
and ugliness of who we are,
living apart but together on the blade of insanity

the beasts still slither among us, their fears
shaped as brutal beliefs and hazy ignorance,
and in your final breaths and thoughts,
I hope you realized a truth more enduring than gold:
the beasts that tortured your innocent body,
could never steal any part of your infinite soul

by Mel Donalson

Emergence

Since we crawled from the earth at Puvuu'nga,
we've plunged headlong
into spindrift,
into frigid Pacific,
fingers combing through tangles of kelp forest
seeking stone and sharp-edged shellfish—
the most sacred of mollusks.
Fingertips graze rock to cup over concave
and columned light gleams through green
revealing ashen, frilling flesh
of abalone.
Plucked from stone-home,
abalone travels with us.
From seafloor, we paddle-kick vertical,
faces racing toward briny surface air and sunlight.
In our emergence,
breath fills our insides
from floating ribs to clavicle.
The sea holds us there buoyant,
and we know the tide
and its tendency to push us back
to the shallows.

by Megan Dorame

the abalone are dying

taking more, taking too much, taking for sport, for sale for food, for expensive food, the most expensive seafood in the world. harvesting, over harvesting, nets over overflow, exploiting, over exploiting, extractive, taking, taking, endangered. warming ocean exhausts expanses of kelp to stump and abalone are starving. endangered, elusive, elusory, existing only in chest or muscle scar, scraped clean with the sweep of the wrist. exhibiting glistering halos fogbows rainbows scalloping outwards in concentric circles and spiraling back to the apex.

by Megan Dorame

What does loss taste like?

Abalone shells ooze from the slippery mouths of infants.

Glistering, mother of pearl mounds are stacked
and stapled to our crowns, their scalloping edges
indenting our foreheads,
and making our hairlines itch.
Our faces, framed phosphorescent, are moth-like
in their senseless propulsion towards the light.

Abalone sunset blazes fluorescent and fades
mercurial, melding
into darkness.

We cup our eyes with abalone shells,
gaze through the curvature of openings
to find the bright of the moon.

Empty shells are infinite as distant stars.
The galaxies, marked by muscle scar,
are the insides of abalone shells.

We string abalone shells around our necks;
let them dangle over our breast for protection.

We nail abalone shells to tree trunks,
hoping to hell to halt harm
from entering our hearths
through breath or arched row of apertures.

In our houses, we cradle bowls made of abalone shell
in the crooks of our elbows,
their blistered exteriors nick at our forearms
tinging our skin with iron and carmine.

With spoons made of abalone shell,
we shovel bits of imagined meat
between our jaws and bite down.
What we chew is grit and glitter midden.
Spitting shell chip, we suckle
the insides of our cheeks,
palates searching for succulent, saltwater flesh.
A flavor so familiar,
it's etched lace-like into mind and tongue.
Instinct moves our mouths in a roundabout motion.
We reel in what's missing by grinding our teeth.
Our grins afflicted
by all that was taken.

by Megan Dorame

Self-Portrait with Favorite Dress

Tonight, I'm thinking of why I don't wear dresses
except occasionally in poems, when I am pretending
to be someone else. I am thinking of why my favorite
dress is a pair of jeans, the color of receding glaciers
or chicory. White-cap blue. In other words,
I like my jeans as faded as possible, worn in places
that correspond to the bones of my body. That phrase,
he'll be buried in his jeans, might apply. Like bones,
they'll be left after the flesh has been turned under,
the smudge of dirt on denim that means I was
working in the garden, taming tomatoes or twisting
the pleated skirts of squash blossoms off their stems
before they could begin to fruit. Perhaps all
dresses are possibility, the swirl of something
else, but my jeans are a line between air and earth,
the evidence of this life, the color of visible wind.

by Linda Dove

What We Share Now

for J, on the occasion of being assigned the same oncologist

Her hands in our bodies, cutting the margins
of flesh around cancer. Pink goo of breast
and entrail, blood greasing the gloves, deft
clips and snips. She is knobbing lymph nodes
in the crook of her thumb and coaxing them
clean of the meat. She is pulling us apart.
She will save us, we believe, we believe.
How many others have shared her fingers
inside them, not counting lovers? It is
like plunging an arm in a lake, breaking
the surface where body disappears into body
to reach for places that never touch air.
The deep pocket of purse that holds the dark.
The coins that swim through the cold.

by Linda Dove

Fifty Years Later

As my corpse drifts beside the riverbed
with one eye open I notice my Maid of Honor
spread lips to pose for photos fifty years later.
Her teeth glow just as they did for my wedding
Today she'll outshine me again. Of course, I'm dead.

Still, I look good as a cadaver. I've swollen
just enough to puff cheeks, fill nasolabial folds,
flatten forehead lines even better than Botox.
I wish someone would take my picture.
Now that I'm dead.

Friends screech how young my sister looks but she's
fifteen years younger than I am/was. She confides
YouTube taught her miracle creams, sliced jade to erase
wrinkles. An inopportune lesson for me since I'm dead.

Sis and bridesmaid lead a conga line, swinging bouquets
of polyester roses and daisies as they boogie and belt
We're goin' to the chapel and we're gonna' get married
as I arranged for *us* to perform at this golden anniversary.
Just my luck I'm dead.

Now they're all singing happy birthday to my husband.
It's mine too but I never celebrate with candles and cake
because I don't want to reveal my sacred number.
If only I had told them, maybe they would sing to me too.
Alone in the cold river, I hope they'll bury my body soon.
I'd rather be rockin' and warblin'. At least I'm here.
But gee whiz, I'm dead!

by Pauline Dutton

cherita comfort

when you find

you are engaged
to a married man

as you munch, wail
drive through the rain
I will be your passenger

when your daughter

marries, moves
to another country

and you sleep in her bed
wear her bunny gown
I will dream of her with you

when you hold her first-born

afraid to care too much
before a soon departure

I will remind you
love never arrives
without a bag of heartache

by Pauline Dutton

My Car Is Like a Woman

You need the right key to turn her on or off

The engine warms up and purrs

.

You have to know what buttons make her blink or honk.
What buttons to cool her off or warm her up.
Taking her convertible top off might not be automatic.
You might have to work on it by hand.
Accelerator: if you push too hard, you could spin your wheels.
For me, I slowly advance from gear-to-gear.
It won't work if you jump into fifth gear when standing still.
Get her going too. You go farther if you don't go too fast.

Otherwise you have an accident of some sort and you
don't drive so long. If you go too long, she runs out of gas,
just as I do. So get off the freeway where it says rest stop.
Also you both could fuel up.

If you take good care of her she lasts longer. If you give
her TLC she works better and looks better.
Come to think of it, my wife has a car too. (a newer model)
I wonder how she would word it.

by Richard Dutton

Previously published in *Spectrum* v. 20, 2019

All The Goodness of the World

I was walking down the street & a woman walking her tiny, tiny dog turned to say *hello dear* & it wasn't the words but her smile— I fell into a hole the size of sweetness & as I fell someone handed me a cup of compassion though it tasted like lemon & honey, & someone handed me joy though it looked like a pink wool hat & when at last I stopped falling, I was back on the street, though it felt as if my feet were standing on white sands in clear water & O the kindness of her eyes— we didn't hug because we were strangers, but I wanted to— her eyes said *it's okay dear*, yes, yes, her eyes said *there is goodness all the days of your life* [as if all the gray-haired grandmothers of the world stood around chanting *hello dear*] & her eyes so brown though they looked like yellow daisies— life handed me grief though it felt like mud & life handed me sadness though it felt like thirst, but in two shakes of a second, here on the street with wild orchids blooming, my heart opened & orange-breasted sparrows followed me home—all because a woman with a tiny, tiny dog has in her secret pockets, secret treats for every living person [not a secret after all]—

by Alicia Elkort

Elegy

A man I don't know lies down in the grass,
his head in a woman's lap,
she rubs his forehead in a slow, circular
motion, her long black hair,
pretty face, his eyes closed—
I think, what a lucky soul, the gingko
leaves rising to the bluest sky—
though a breeze too warm, the park
is alive with children & picnics.
I'm walking slowly
having just read about the journalist
who was murdered—they cut off his fingers
one by one—what I'm trying to say,
I'm finding it terribly difficult
to hold these two realities inside
of myself. In a world with many hells,
I have found my own kind of peace,
but my mind is ablaze with a man
I've never met, never heard of until today
& I can't stop crying, justice
is some kind of magical word
that shows up for some of us
but not many & his face—
his face—in my mind, I am rubbing
his temples, praying for love, holding—
I'm holding his head & my hands are burning,
there's so much fire, the pain
is too much—I run to the fountain,
drop my hands in the water—

what I'm asking is why are we so brutal
when it's simple to create joy?
Sing with me now, raise your voice—
before nightfall, the body leaves a shadow.

by Alicia Elkort

Dark Sky

Your words are as exquisite as
The most beautiful star above me
You shine brightly
Your love drips on me
I stand under
Catching your whispers
On my tongue
Pour yourself into my mouth
So I can swallow all of you
And be filled by you
Once and for all
Only then will I find contentment
Under your dark sky

by Dawn Robin English

purple love

Purple garden surprises
Mark the magic of our soil
Fairy glitter and lightning

We plant buckwheat and ceanothus
For the pollinators
There's a mischievous mint

Creeping into the shadow,
It just wants to stay cool
It has purple flowers too

Somehow all our plants have
Purple flowers
From the violas to the natives

To the cabbages and cauliflowers
Your sweat crafted layers of soil
Like a seedling I tuck myself

In your earth soaked arms
Watered with love and wonder
Seed, root, soil entwined

Red and pink poppies emerge
Our hearts beat close to the ground
We blossom and glow in purple love

by Lynn Fang

Rocks

Five ordinary rocks she gave me
Unwrapped, uneven, soil clinging
Ordinary rocks not at all

by Lynn Fayne

A poem I gathered

If I could coax and take apart
A poem's tangled strands
To find and formulate
Its definition
And hold them blithely in my hands

Here, in the moonlight
Under midnight's mossy glow
Where conjurers practice
Their black arts
Would I gather
Poem components and poem subparts
That I may come to know
What a poem is
Comprised of
What its being has to show

From
Images and themes
Sounds mutedloud and schemes
For rhyme and meter
All the in betweens
Of salty lemon thyme
And other overtones
A single joysorrow tear iambically displayed
Where fields of broken
Like carnage laid
With bones and
Multi under umber tones

That balance on the edge
About to teeter
Held together
With
The mortar of the unsaid
To
What that poet must have meant
With each clearopaque word condiment
Supplying daily bread,
All wiped thoroughly
With isopropyl alcohol
Applied with scrupulously
Clean hands
Gatherings all analyzed
And laid out antiseptically
As a bill of particulars
Leaving cleaved apart
And helpless
Poemessence mystery

by Lynn Fayne

Fleshing out a rectangle

On the Sanborn map*

Codes, roads, what it cost
All this and more is mostly lost
Except to some librarians
 Antiquarians urbanarians
And those who think that
They can still remember

Those that shoveled soil
With concrete rebar did the toil
And laid foundations
For structures reaching skyward

To house an office factory or store
In which to make or sell or process
Something with receipt

So that a family could eat
A family whose members
Did not know what came before

A taking did occur
Within this domain
So eminent

Whether compensation
Was just or not
Was swept away just

Like the razed and rusty rebar
Mixed with broken
Concrete shards and rubble

And removed by someone
With payment for their trouble

by Lynn Fayne

*digital file of LA Vol 2 1923-53
  From the Sanborn Map Collection

Battleground

How do you approach
the battleground where you lost?
The ashes are cold. Flowers now bloom
between the black bones of broken trees.
Why even go back? Better to let the grass
grow over the blood of ghosts.

But we all go back.

Do bodies crave pain? Or maybe
we want to find the hope that was lost
when the shrieking fell to its silence.
Its echo follows us like a feral bitch
barking at our heels. Maybe we need
to return the echo, give it a proper burial.
And what is a proper burial? How many veils
do you need? How big must the tombstone be?
And how do you stop it from being exhumed,
a scar ripped open like a mouth?

How do you return
to the battleground where you lost?

Do you go alone, late at night,
under a sky so cloudy, stars can't
shine through with their piercing eyes
of possibility? Do you go with lovers,
their arms around your waist,
holding you up in the hot sun

so you can tear away
from them, their support a suffocation?

Maybe you shouldn't.

Maybe you must. Go there, fall on your knees,
take the soft ash in your hands, you must.
Rub it into your eyes, cake it on your cheeks.
Let your tears carve new paths
in a face that has turn to stone.
However you choose,
                    you must.

by Emily Fernandez

Sorry No Apocalypse

New Year's Day 2017

The decorations hang from the rafters
waiting to catch fire and drop ash on us,
the revelers and wasted, clasping our fingers
but the bright paper flowers will not have closure,
only collect dust, shiver slightly in the breeze,
slowly fade to grey.

We are tired of talking about the apocalypse,
we have nothing more to prep, beyond ready,
we've stopped lighting candles
or burning incense and sage.
We are on our knees, pleading,
with old clothes, and old stories,
same wants and needs, unheard,
but there will not be a burning sky
or a voice from above striking us
with a tongue through our heart.
We wait for the new year holding our breath
with blue lips and red eyes.
We look at each other with our faces
drooping from our skull like skin we need to lose.
Waiting.

Someone will have to break the knife on the bread gone stale,
and laugh our way back to love and struggle again
in this same old stupid world.

by Emily Fernandez

Garlic

right wing racist
gun boner in hand waving it aloft
Moloch in the chamber Moloch for the 2nd
who walked the alleys of the Internet
filling their pockets with stochastic terror
insisting
who must respect their irrelevance
do not speak to me
without blood

Moloch in the House
swagger and strut
and shepherd their flock of thoughts and prayers
out onto the common
to display
begging for their participation trophies
and honorable mentions
Moloch who demanded
        – silence

Moloch in the Senate
fawning over the eggshell egos
that still vote for them
waiting for the rotted organs
transplanted
beating with the rhythm
of two masters
Moloch in the bullet Moloch in the Press
an incarnation of the fallacy of balance

an avatar
on some NRA version of Grindr

and I am with you
      – in Gilroy
as America is torn tattered untreated
in some star spangled insanity of self abuse
as mourning comes a new day
I am with you

by Mark Fisher

Mojave

empty miles of sand and stone
and hidden wildflower seeds
where twisted Joshua Trees
cast their shadows onto
the dry and dusty memories
of the seas they used to be
as ravens imagine they're seagulls
calling to the mirage's waves
washing across desert varnished basalt
covered in petrogylphs
whispering stories in forgotten languages
from before the awareness of gold
drew the tsunami
and the flotsam of the storm
leaving holes and metal cans
across the desert bed
now crossed with off-road scars
in torn up creosote
and still years are piling up
as the faults slowly move
while the desert dreams
it's a sea
once again

by Mark Fisher

Crossing

the helicopter flashed its lights

down we went under a bush
the mud hugged our feet
as if the earth itself was embracing us

whispering,
"i won't let them take you"

i needed to pee
i needed our coyote to take me in his arms
and place me upon his shoulders

i held it in
the urine
the tears

only two hours to San Diego
where the warm water would caress my skin
and my mom would invite the hotel shampoo and soap
to join us in our journey to Los Ángeles

by Oombi Solis Flores

Previously Published: *Razorcake* #102 – February 2018, *My Mouth Tastes Like Horchata* – March 2017

Falling

petals fall
from my skin
softly set flight

ticklish petals

they ride out
the waves
taking their time

underneath
a new skin
grows

soft pink
light brown

no longer
ticklish

i let u
in

the petals
fall

i let u
in

by Oombi Solis Flores

Tucson, AZ

From a hint of rich green rot
I smell the grass before I see it
Amid the clean desert breezes
Overwrought moisture
Tells me of nearby lawns
For golf
Not of earth
Nor the local sages
But of civilization playing at Eden

by Katherine Footracer

Insulin Blues

Cold, sweaty, and shaking
2:52 a.m.
I'm 50
Walk to the kitchen to check
Nobody but the dog is watching
But I still try not to flinch
Everything hurts more near 3 a.m.
Grab the colorless shot glass
With markings that used to be red
Open the fridge
Down a slug of sweetness
Then settle in to wait
I'm not hungry but I think about what I can eat
Not a PBJ
Maybe crackers with cheese
Chocolate ice cream from the freezer
But I can't share that with the dog
Who deserves a treat for hanging with me
When I wake low-sugared in the night

by Katherine Footracer

Pray Thee to Anacreon in Heaven*
(A Green Stained Knee)

It was a knee, a grass stained knee
No grand Tommy Smith -John Carlos
Victory stand fisted, black gloved salute

No flip the bird or mooning the moon
It was a knee, a green grass stained knee
A silent, nonviolent, protesting knee

In a contested view of a freedom song
Sung all wrong--Land of the white free
Grave to the black slave—it was a knee

A symbolic dissent to the dreaded Scott
Decision: No rights need be respected—
Defiantly rejected, refusing to be a knave

Totally aware of the camera's red glare
Irate fan boos bursting the pre-game air
Refusing to be a slave, he took a knee

by GT Foster

*The Anacreontic Song was the title of the toasting tune to which Francis Scott Key's poem In Defense of Fort McHenry was written. In 1931, as The Star Spangled Banner, it became the United States national anthem.

Elementary Art

In the wind, palm trees sway,
letting go of old fronds.
their burnished pelvises with long dry leaves
that look like the hair of the drowned
dive to the street.

Once after a storm,
for my nephew's third grade art class,
a parent brought in a wagon of fronds
for the kids to decorate
with red, green and yellow paint.

His piece hangs like a giant ancient arrow
on my sister's living room wall,
bold and avant-garde.
She is reminded of his early promise
when the world was bright and young.

Now he's a cop on long night shifts
traveling into hardscrabble lives:
the homeless, gangs, drugs, violence.
He can barely recall
his youthful dream of heroism
or how simple pleasures were.

But sometimes after a rain
when the mean streets are washed clean,
he remembers playing on the porch

with dump trucks and fire engines,
skateboarding on the sidewalk,
a rainbow over his childhood.

by Joyce Futa

Memento

The beauty of some things is unexpected:
the rose, for instance, that Liz gave me
from her mother's memorial bouquet,
an ordinary, perfect hothouse rose,
giant, pink, half open.

I thought it would wilt quickly
but began to notice
it was exquisite for a long time,
never dropping its petals,
wafting a honey fragrance.
Gradually it dried with curled red edges
like parchment.

I thought of Tonia and how she aged
so quickly and painfully her last year.
In gaunt old age she trembled,
but smiled now and then
with a determined radiance.
She didn't go willingly.

I went about my daily routines,
thought of her when I looked at the rose.
After a month I cut off its long stem
and put it, fragrance faded,
into a small clay cup of memory.

by Joyce Futa

Pantoum

If my father wrote poems I would know his thoughts
I dream as I wake, shrouded from light,
write as I wake repeating lines
sometimes the days are like a dream

I dream as I wake, shrouded from light
the wife washing dishes and row, row the boat
sometimes the days are like a dream
birds singing in trees, things in the stores

the wife washing dishes and row, row the boat
nights are hard work, soliloquies circle
birds singing in trees, things in the stores
now shrouded in silence while I am awake

nights are hard work, soliloquies circle
I punch into pillows, peaceful dog at my feet
shrouded in silence while I am awake
I read about children and the end of the world

I punch into pillows, peaceful dog at my feet
when my son dreams of me, he sails right on by
I read about children and the end of the world
one day he will stop and what will he think

if my father wrote poems I would know his thoughts

by Joyce Futa

A Monologue with Mom

Mom, I'm missing you a lot.
Do you miss me, too? I hope you do but without feeling sad.
Tell me, is heaven really the way we thought it was?
Is God sitting around a cloud of beautiful shiny lights?
Are Angels singing while playing harps?
Are there many beautiful, green apple trees?
Dad loved Red Delicious; do you remember?
He said he'd eat apples in Paradise.
Sometimes I think I'm ready for us to meet again;
I'm just not ready to die and leave my daughter.
I wish you could've met her;
you would've loved her, and she you.
You would've made a great grandmother,
unlike the one I had.
Good thing my daughter met grandpa, too.
Both spent time together reading books.
He'd read her "The Three Little Pigs."
It was in English, but neither seemed to mind.
Do you talk to dad again? I hope you do.
I know you loved each other despite the silence.
Now you have time to make up for lost years.
Put pride aside and give him a chance;
he did the best he could.
Ask him if he's hungry.
He'll tell you he wants some beans.
You'll ask him, "How many?"
-Unos tres, he'll say.
Then you'd count, one, two, three!
And we'd all burst out laughing; do you remember that?

I know things could've been better for all.
I could've been a better daughter,
and no excuse can change things now;
I'm reaping what I sowed, not what I meant.
My tears can't change my rebellious past,
but I had no vices to blame things on;
it was the hand life dealt me.
I hope you found peace and have no regrets.

by Martina Gallegos

Mother's Womb

Life ends when death begins
in the journey of the sacred
womb of Mother Earth.
Mother Earth begins the cleansing
of the body it just welcomed
back to its loving arms.
Now the child begins a new life
cradled with love and integrity
before sharing it with the world.
The new child wonders
whether it's worth leaving
such nurturing nest.
No worries, no dangers,
only love and affection
Mother Earth humbly offers.
Life and death are part of life,
and death eventually turns to life,
so we live it with Mother Earth.

by Martina Gallegos

First published by *Poets Responding to SB1070*, October 25, 2016.

 RAINBOW

The smile of a child in tattered clothes
The injured bird that keeps flying
The friend who never forgets
That mother who keeps on loving
The poor who keeps giving
Sun-rays that push through clouds
Clouds that cry tears of joy
And the fields that greet them.
 Rainbow that persists
And resists rejection
And showers with loving colors
Nature's creatures and
People's hands
That feed us
 Rainbow that mocks
The hummingbird
As it hovers over gardens
And flowers hidden amongst it.
 Rainbow playing across the skies
Saying goodbye to showers
And leaving Planet Earth
A heartfelt peace

by Martina Gallegos

First published in *Poets Responding to SB1070*, February 9th, 2019.

Joey Jams Jazz Chords
in the Urban Schoolyard

Blues, not so much a smoggy skyline
but white-bloused uniforms
and acrylic, snap-on ties,
on a vaporous school-day
morning.

Joey and his pals rehearse
like thirteen-year-olds would:
missed notes, sour vocals,
and ill-formed chords,
while four-square balls thump
counter-beats in the schoolyard.

La Bamba just wasn't his thing.
Stones and Beatles maybe
but Joey wanted to play Jazz.
—blue notes,
improvisation,
polyrhythms
and syncopation.

Joey was cool,
atypical of those
pop loving,
gum smacking,
junior high school students.

He was so cool,

his friends didn't understand
the fake Ray-Ban® shades
and his Beatnik lingo
or his triad transpositions
during that hot September
in 1966.

by Jerry Garcia

Suburban Recessional

Men dressed like funerals
emerge from evergreen hedges
to outfit jacaranda trees in black tie.
Cats herd onto sidewalks singing *In Paradisum*,
children float Popsicle-stick rafts
in gutter-water streams.
Palm fronds bow like acolytes
to wrinkled elders pushing shopping carts.
Barbecues create multiple plumes of suburban incense as crows chorus
benediction.

Clouds are cirrus and loose,
jet condensation tracks blue spaces,
shadows make the sign of the cross
on upswept sidewalks.
Nuns pray in blue wardrobe
on every street corner.

The mailman passes with the redemption
of John the Baptist along the way
to losing his head.

by Jerry Garcia

Previously published "On Summer Solstice Road" by Jerry Garcia, *Green Tara Press* ©2016

There are things you don't have to inherit

Your mother's teacups, for instance
It's okay not to love them
and to drop them off at the local thrift store.
When you pack up her house, it's okay to save
the wine-colored sweater she cuddled you in,
the mixer that made chocolate cakes
on rainy afternoons.
It's okay to throw out the dusty menorah
and the way she stared hatefully at her image in the mirror,
that laser that began
with her cold father and beamed straight
into her young body, out her eyes, and into you.
When packing up her house, it's okay
to drape her old sheets over the long mirrors,
pull her heavy front door closed behind you,
and buy new mirrors for your own home,
to look into them each morning as the coffee pot gurgles
and say to yourself, hello there.
Hello.

by Catherine Gewertz

Mother Nature dances with
man-not-so-kind

Man dances with nature
He encircles her swaying
Slow and steady
Fast and spirited
He leads with his arms
She leads with her eyes

One leading the other
As the song progresses
So does the intensity of his grasp
It moves from hand-in-hand to fingers on pulse

As she struggles for air
He tightens his hold
Pierces her skin with his nails
She grabs ahold of his arm
She could claw back
She could gouge out his eyes
She could take hold of where it hurts the most
Instead, thinking of her children, tears flow and she musters up the
strength to yell
At the top of her lungs "I love you"

He embraces her tight
Wraps his fingers into her hair even tighter
And swiftly pulls back as hard as he can
Her neck snaps back to receive the kiss

The dance slows
Her pulse quiets
He carries nothing but a corpse
No rhythm
No dance
No life

by Luz Gutierrez

Mother nature calls for help

Mother nature begs to be heard
She cries rivers
Lakes
Oceans

She pours her heart out in storms
Hurricanes
Tornadoes

She quakes strong and furious
To wake us from our slumber
To alert us to her slow suffocation

To our indifference she rages a blaze
Hoping that her heat warms our hearts
Warms us to her cries for help
Warms us to her cries for help
Warns us to help

by Luz Gutierrez

Mushroom Hunters

Downer
amazing

visited Hiroshima
where a mushroom cloud
turned an entire city
into a graveyard—
prayed for peace...
called up down in New Orleans
under a bad moon when Hurricane Katrina
submerged Crescent City beneath flood waters
and reborn mushrooms came marching in...
passed out meals and medicine for the Red Cross
ripped mold-encrusted carpet and drywall for FEMA
while The Big Easy, rising again, dried out slowly...
toured Chernobyl where radioactive
mushrooms still glow in darkness...
considered my blessed innocent bystander students
killed in drive-bys by gangbangers who mocked them
as "Mushrooms" because they "popped up" on sidewalks...
remembered decomposing corpses
in Vietnam jungles cloaked in fungus fur
monsoon mushrooms blossoming from decaying skin...
pondered how a tiny rifle bullet mushroomed
to blow out a president's skull....

declared war against mushrooms
fought the virulent fungi
my private campaign against champignons
growing on the fields of Mars...
ate them raw in salads
devoured them cooked in soups

114

polished them off on pizza
ingested them in spaghetti sauces
consumed them in exotic casseroles
feasted on them gathered wild in forests
forgot my *Edible Fungus Guide*...
popped one in my mouth to sample the taste
fatal mistake— "Destroying Angel" toxic toadstool...
died alone miles from the nearest road
hallucinogenic visions of reincarnation buzzing my brain...
when we hunt mushrooms, mushrooms we become—
then the mushrooms ate me....

by Charles Harmon

Retired Senryu Sequence

retired
emphasis
on the second syllable

results
may vary
DNA

that's the way
the cookie crumbles
(my fortune)

a day in the life of a mayfly

telephone tag
postponing
the inevitable

never buried
Einstein's brain
still thinking outside the box

cormorant fisherman
feeling a ring
around their own necks

haiku
my rosary beads
my Prozac

just remember
it's all a simulation
spaceship windows

washing her hands
for the millionth time
Lady Macbeth

by Charles Harmon

Previously published in *frogpond*, (1, 2, 3) Winter, Summer, Fall 2019;
autumn moon, (4) 6/2019;
bottle rockets, (5) August, 2019*: prune juice*, (6) July, 2019; *ephemerae*, (7, 8)
Spring 2019;
Haiku Foundation Dialogue, (9) June, 2019; *akitsu*, (10) Summer 2019

Bomb Crater Kyoka Sequence

welcome committee
makes you feel right at home
friendly, at ease
but what's with the pitchforks?
and why's it so damned hot?

he holds up
seven missing fingers
mumbles "Korea"
I give him an elbow bump
with what's left of my arm

she thinks
my scars look badass
good thing
she can't see the ones
hidden deep inside

playing sad violin
standing in the bomb crater
wanting to believe
lightning never strikes twice
in the same place

under a low sky
grayness presses down
on my spirit—
longing to see bright stars
I create them out of mind

it all comes down
to chemistry
the proton's attracted
by the electron's symmetry
that little flash in the pan…

by Charles Harmon

Previously published in *Atlas Poetica*: (1) # 35 November, 2018; (2) #36
February, 2019;
(3, 4, 5) #37 May, 2019; (6) #38 September, 2019

Listen

What happens if we sit in silence
Maybe God can come in
We often bring so much noise
Sometimes we bring so many people
He can't come in
Even if He's there whispering
We can't hear we don't hear
Make it impossible to hear
Fill our minds stuff our ears
Cram our souls with things
Crowding God out
When God wants to talk
He wants us to be silent and
Listen
If we are to hear
We must not bring so much noise
Bring so many people
Sometimes we wiggle and squirm
Often we are impatient try to
Summon God on our terms
The struggle we lose still we try
We have to learn
Quiet the noise silence the people
Restrain our voice calm our hearts
Be still Be still Be still
When God wants to talk
He wants us to be silent and
Listen

by Shirley Harris

Don't Leave Without Saying Goodbye

Don't leave without saying goodbye
Say we don't see eye to eye
Say you loved me but now it's gone
Now we can both move along
Fill the void with the words of ending
not the drama of pretending
fill my heart with words of concluding
not the charade of calm eluding
don't just walk and let me wonder
I'm not in danger of going under
Don't want much just something decisive
There's no need to be divisive
Dragging it out is no act of benevolence
It may turn out to be malevolence
Say it's been fun but I have to go
Say you've been kind but not my show
Say you're really not the one for me
Say I have somewhere else to be
Say it's been good and you've been nice
We won't pass this way – not twice
Evasion gives us nothing to gain
I can always stand the pain
Ease the ache with simple finality
A final dose of our reality
Say I'm sorry I changed my mind
Say I never meant to be unkind
Don't' leave without saying goodbye
I promise you I won't cry

by Shirley Harris

Hands Up Don't Shoot!

We raise our hands
but it don't matter

POW! POW! POW!
Bullets fly

We run
Trey fall down
I hear his mama cry

Hands up don't shoot!

In movies hands up
means surrender

Cops handcuff rebels
take them to jail

But for us the same rules
don't apply

Whether our hands
are up or down
we die.

by Hazel Clayton Harrison

Previously published in *Down Freedom Road*, Shabda Press, 2020

Summer Haiku

Tipuana tree
stop shedding your flowers
I'm tired of sweeping.

By the door
a lonely rocking chair waits
for me to sit down.

A corpulent bee
lying in a flower bed
Is it drunk or dead?

Near the beach
carved in stone, a turtle head
points to the sea.

by Hazel Clayton Harrison

The Haenyeo (Women of the Sea)
(for mothers who make great sacrifices to educate their daughters)

For generations they were the bread winners of
Jeju Island

Without breathing gear, they dove into the Korea
Strait holding their breaths, harvesting seafood

Poor and illiterate, they swam like fish in schools
carrying their coffins on their backs*

Under her blue-green waves, Mother Sea nourished them
with her abalone and algae

When pregnant, the sea women dreamed of delivering
their babies in Mother Sea's arms

In times of sorrow, salt from their tears mingled with hers
When Grandmother Seoulmundae** heard them weeping

she spilled lava over the island until school officials
opened their doors for her daughters

The sea women had to dive deeper to pay school fees
          but now their daughters are educated

They do not have to dive carrying coffins on their backs
like their mothers

The sea women are now grandmothers. Soon they will
disappear, but today they still plunge into the sea

holding their breaths, harvesting seafood, happy to
sink into Mother Sea's embrace.

by Hazel Clayton Harrison

*Phrase the Haenyeo use to describe net sacks they carry on their backs
when diving
**Mother Creator, the Haenyeo's name for Mount Halla

Previously published in *Down Freedom Road*, Shabda Press, 2020

Seism

sometimes my hands tremble

like those of an old, arthritic gentleman.
there's no romance
in flitting fingertips that strain to assemble

orderly ranks and cram
themselves into a semblance of meaning.
(to form coherent movement
is to translate coherent thought.)

my hands are my tells
and I'm losing the game of composure.
each wild quiver

unearths the tremors of my mind, its wells
where quavering voices
echo: "what next?" I have no answer,

so my hands will tremble.

by Eleanor Harvey

floral demoiselles

some are orchids—
decked in luscious purples and regal whites,
silken stems arched
like reclining revellers on wild nights,
as each petal, imbued
with heady perfume, beguiles and delights.

some are sunflowers—
bronze florets framed by an auroral ring
of sun-soaked yellow
that spin in leisurely circles and cling
to fading warmth,
like sunbathers, tanning for a summer fling.

some are snowdrops—
chaste white bells bowing tenderly to kiss
the frosted earth,
thawing inhibitions and awakening bliss;
an innocent, adored,
yet shrouded in snow, a frigid abyss.

some are poppies—
alluringly poised and clothed in carnal red;
ruby femmes fatales,
that tempt enraptured lovers to be wed
to opium seeds
which numb, as passion gently turns to dread.

by Eleanor Harvey

Democracy, Democracy

Democracy, democracy,
have we taken you for granted for too many years,
neglected our history,
forgotten lives lost so you could survive,
left you unmaintained, un-groomed,
a breeding ground for weeds of fascism to sprout?

Are the masses too blind
to see what's growing right in front of their eyes?
Do they look through the eye of a needle,
unable to see consequences of their desires?

Democracy, democracy,
have we become so complacent
we no longer know who you are?
What happened after 200 years,
the rules so mis-comboggled
that the minority rules?

Now we've created an atmosphere
where there's no middle ground.
How do we find balance,
peace, create minds that are sound?

Democracy, democracy,
have we born a nation of I, I, Me, Me,
where no one can see
outside the confines of their own lives?
Do we know anymore, what democracy is?
Will we remember, before our demise?

by Teri Hicks

Homeless Man

Strung out on drugs,
a means to cope with life,
unable to decipher reality from illusion,
he accepts what is,
embraces his addiction,
apologizes to no one,
not even himself.

In our reality, he's homeless.
In his reality,
he lives in the present,
moves his treasured filled bags in a shopping cart,
home is wherever he stops.
We look at him,
wonder how miserable he must be.

He lives and accepts his life as is.
No worries of what has past
or what is to come.
He smiles, laughs, dances on the sidewalk
to a beat only he can hear.
He roams in another dimension
happy and fancy free.

What's good for him
may not be good for you or me.
We see his reality as an illusion.
He may very well be living a life of freedom
that we cannot see.

Whose illusion?
Whose reality?

by Teri Hicks

Questions for the Gods

Dear God, Heavenly Father, The Infinite One,
Father God, Yahweh, Allah, Grandfather, Tunkashila,
Wakantanka, Great Spirit, Great Mystery,
Jehovah, Creator, Supreme Being, The Almighty,
You, who are known by a thousand names and a thousand places,
You, the Alpha and Omega,
Creator and Knower of all that is,

If I am in You and You are in me,
if we are all one
then what is the purpose
of hatred, war and greed?

We take up arms,
destroy cities and lives,
tell me Heavenly Father,
why, from generation to generation,
this continues to go on and on?

The loss of a son, a daughter
fighting for a country,
Tunkashila, tell me
what does that really mean?
The atrocities we inflict upon one another are unfathomable to me.

What would the people of this country do
if we were invaded by strangers dressed in helmets and boots,
with guns and grenades slung on their chest,
riding in hum-v's, tanks and military trucks,

131

destroying homes, museums, whole communities,
eradicating livelihoods, our way of life, our way of being?

We think we're the good guys and they're the bad ones,
they think we're bad and they're the good ones.
Who is who and what is what,
Yahweh, Allah, Wankantanka,
can you reveal the truth to us?

Great Spirit,
if I am in You and You are in me,
if we are all one,
then why all these wars
and so much senseless death?

Dear God, Creator,
please hear my plea,
fix us, awaken us, help us to see,
change us, so that we all feed the Collective
that brings to this world, Love, Peace and Harmony.

by Teri Hicks

Grandmother's House

Dingy white clapboard house
cracked porch stair
ledge with terracotta pot and tin watering can
heavy wooden screen door screeches, bangs
mighty oak front door with four beveled panes

Beyond the threshold
the great room   cast in shadow
sunbeams stream through north face window
spills on floral tapestry of wingback chair
where she gathers for devotion
kneels down in dutiful prayer;
her Bible lain open
God's   words   spoken

Chandelier weeps crystal tiers
dining table draped in lace
a vase of fresh cut roses from her front yard garden
Built-ins, a shrine for fine bone china
display gold rimmed Wedgwood plates
Lismore Lace teacups and saucers,
an ornate maple hutch
holds silver, linen

Scents of her southern roots infiltrate pastel rooms
fatback, collard greens, hot water cornbread,
a tin of peach cobbler deep enough to swim in
from stone fruit preserves
her busied hands canned

All such morsels of love
simmered in a cast iron skillet
her heavy aproned breasts before the stove
in the bright yellow kitchen
where, there, after grace
we dine on her down home cookin'
beneath an oblong framed Jesus
poised at the "Last Supper"

by Andria Hill

The Visit

Locked inside
Trapped outside
wondering are you okay
this mystery has me questioning,
what's the point

She's seated at the table
her fingers, not her thumb, in her mouth
no plate, spoon, fork or knife
only crumbs an empty black coffee cup
she holds to her mouth licking the rim

She's in a triad-world memory drought
embellished gibbering childlike laughter
   fixed sensations of touch and feel
         flashing realities
         she rubs the floor
   investigates the wall from her chair

She's shifting into new levels of reality
      last week, told her my name
       she repeated my name
         she said, my son
      overjoyed, on cloud nine
         she remembered
      and next time will be next time.......

by Randel Horton

Dignified Burials

*for African migrants (who drowned in the Mediterranean Sea
trying to reach Europe.* Against resistance to foreigners who are not Muslim*

Two red brick columns mark
crowded stadium size cemetery
mostly unmarked makeshift

graves surrounded
by olive groves
garbage from town dump

In southern Tunisia bodies
washed ashore since 2000
Marzoug laid hundreds to rest

Most migrants buried from
Africa Sudan Somalia Nigeria
Ivory Coast no ID.

Marzoug began identifying
graves with numbers on
body bag bracelets.

Believes he is there to watch over
and protect them by providing
dignified burials.

by Gerda Govine Ituarte

*Molly Hennessy-Fiske, "Tunisian makes it his mission to bury migrants
lost to sea," *Los Angeles Times*, November 27, 2017.

Thanks Giving

Family fingerprints present pull me back to the round-robin gatherings on different
occasions or "just because." Aunt Rosa Uncle Stephen's wife, invited the family
for Thanksgiving dinner. I was a pre-teenager with books in tow. Knew where
to find a quiet place to read undisturbed. My cousins knew they could not
coax me to go outside to play. When we arrived the turkey was frozen
with no dinner at-the-ready. To make it easier for everyone, Mom put
Aunt Rosa in bed so she could "sleep it off"-- the alcohol she drank
prior to and during our visit. I was uncomfortable and had never
seen anyone in a state of disarray and confusion. My Mom and
four Aunties went into "let's take care of this now mode," an
organized army of strong personalities. They checked to
see what was in the pantry—made a shopping list. Two
went to the store while the others started preparing.
Within hours a full course dinner was on the table
with all the trimmings. My family did not make a
fuss. They turned chaos on its head as our feast
continued with the usual jokes, disagreements
and "digs" while jockeying for more "air time."

by Gerda Govine Ituarte

LP Record

Skipping at the same spot
If you had Alzheimer
You, who became drunk noisy last night and
Decent I, who just woke-up peacefully in late afternoon
We must be the same person

Folded it up old,
Where   fine needles of memory cracked
Where the gorge becomes desolate

I raise my hand to reach my back
the blind spot
Where we must raise flowers
Never meet each other
Blind and deaf
So many of us
Gone finely wrong

We were immature and earnest and pathetic
Cloud on the mountain couldn't come down
In some spring equinox

by Ellice Jeon

Late, Spring

Falling cherry blossoms in the corner of a room
White powder and nightmares
Covered ears
Frontline
Hallucinating night

Through his cigarette smoke
Come the soldiers of Falluja
The Red Mother who chopped off the blooms,
Follows his neck in apparition

Each day, too lethargic to be grabbed tightly,
Pierced through the constrained body

He aims for the apparition of the souls,
Who were aiming at him
Rigid eyes of fading late spring disperses in a long line on
The banister of the apartment

by Ellice Jeon

To Scatter at Descanso Gardens

Cuando yo me muera,
enterradme si queris en una veleta.
Cuando yo me muera! ~ *Lorca*

When evening arrives
as a stranger in velvet slippers
it has no shadow
    but you panic
at your mirrored reflection
in the dark.
It feels like death—
a spider waiting
and when you leave
    this body
it will weave you
into forgetting.
But you want to remember all
    you've ever been
a Buddha beneath
the Bodhi tree.
Watch your lives
    burn away
like a great forest
    then the calm
        the ash.
Sebastián the gardener says
    he'll find you again,
when he's troweled
the upper fields

and dug the weeds away.
　He'll talk to you
so you'll never be lonely.
He knows how deer leap
　　　the fence
in the closed hours
to graze on the sweetest grasses.
　　How the ghosts
of the scrub oaks wander.
There are nights
when the moon slips off
　　its white coat
and every wild thing
stirs in its cauldron.
When the wind rattles
　the leaves
you'll be buried like Lorca
in a weather vane—
the one that stands
near the fiery maple
　　how it turns and turns
toward the stars
cold with memory.

by Lois P. Jones

✓

Way
more / minute
than

To a Friend at Rilke's Grave in Raron

Alles ist eins. ~ Rilke

for Lia

The black-faced sheep
  are bleating, their bells
a soft song—a clinking of spoons
  in tin cups—a call to presence
when the world draws them
  into its map of the living.
The pines trees know how the dark hum
  of a new season enters the lungs
like a promise. And if it is a promise
  how can it be sustained?
I stand in bare feet near my rucksack
  and the grey slate path
to his grave. The mountains offer distance,
  the snow a memory of a life
I barely recall. Just the blue repeating
  of the Alps and from somewhere a chant—
three words that fall from the air
  as my shadow touches his grave.
And as I whisper them over and over
  I cannot say he isn't present.
I cannot say the dead don't move toward
  what calls them. Only how the valley stretches
its worn jacket on the grass
  and begs me to stay. How my heart
is a spinnaker in the wind
  catching the breath of it. I linger as long

as I can—until the shadow of his cross
        escapes into darkness. I make my way back
through the mosaic of gravestones
        and the plots of bright flowers planted
near each grave. Cross the corner
        where the aspen trembles
and then I see you just as you are—awoken
        from the place of dreams and I cannot tell where
the soft green slope of the hill ends
        and your hip begins. I want to say
don't forget her, she's still on the hill,
        her body shaded from October sun—
her face in profile, arms resting on knees
        as she looks into the deepening vale.
Aren't parts of us buried in the lands we meet?
        Our souls broken into bones
sure as flint. There are foxes like wood smoke
        in the body. They move quietly in the forest.
They know one of their own. They will find you.
        They will dig you up.

by Lois P. Jones

Leafless Eve

Standing tall on the hillside,
I lift my dark limbs
through a blue wind-whipped sky.

No more life-giving juice
runs under my bark.
No feathered nests on my breasts.

From the first breaking dawn
I've borne leaves, cones, and fruits
that breezes rocked gently to sleep.

Bereft of my green leafy crown,
stripped of former beauty,
my years giving shade are past.

In my flexible and naïve youth,
my supple arms branched
out and touched all four winds.

Now I no longer bend to every whim,
but stand sturdy, defiant and strong
against history's blustering tales.

Remember me not
for elegant grace, cooling shade,
or the peaches I bore,

but revere rugged strength,
and the knowledge I've gleaned
on my gardenless mountain crest.

by Lorelei Kay

Attending My Former Lover's Wedding

Before the long-robed
priest they stand,
all smiles,

my ex-lover
and his soon-to-be
new bride.

Yet moments before
the ceremony began, he
confessed to me his feet

felt icy cold, and at any
moment might skedaddle
for the hills.

But chilled or not,
instead of fleeing,
they inch their way

languidly up the aisle
toward the wooden
altar.

During *our* many years
together, he chose hiking
mountain tops over

attending mass, and
outdoor vistas over
sacramental wafers.

He also chuckled gleefully
at the grandiloquent
hats he'd seen perched

flamboyantly atop
hallowed heads at any
high and holy mass.

Until her.

Now he kneels piously
at his own wedding mass,
before the priest who speaks

with an accent he's
declared, "too foreign
to understand."

His home hosts their
reception, showcasing
his pride of bachelorhood—

moose brass lamps, bear
pictures, and rugs running
perpetually amuck

bearing tracks
of moose, deer,
and elk.

Not only his manly
cave, but his manly
Shangri-La.

All because he said "I do,"
he now has Mary Ann
residing in his bedroom,

and a three-and-a-half-foot
statue of the Virgin Mary
presiding in his living room.

The moose, bears, and elk
paw restlessly, all glaring
at these new intruders.

With two new women
moving in, how many
of *them* might soon

be forced to move on out?

by Lorelei Kay

A Pasadena Sidewalk Cafe

The 256 bus grinds by, accelerates a rubber scent
or diesel breath paste onto the place,
rust orange purple glue that holds
together

automotive motion with garden quietude.
Here we pretend from the overhanging
palm grapes & succulent
brides

an oasis or forest. Here we erase five p.m.
traffic to watch from book-lifted eyes
a wooden fence layered over with
dittany dust,

hear soft dialogue & ice click the edge
of glass. This is culture: people
gathering at tables
surrounded

by cacti, people rarely gesturing through
smogged plant exude (Phylogenetics
all rush protest. Enough of it
faults the road).

Warm November unties itself from the sun
for sauntering. Laptops open epiphanies
for singles while couples draw
through wide

colored straws refreshment: gold tubes
borrow thinly, The chain pole look at the
entrance into the café garden,
straw thin halts

influx by chain fastened. Hanging pearls:
palm fruit retreats behind clay, set where
poems by Municipal Code are
against the law

as are Sunday poetry readings. Today is
wind cooing to palm branches, inviting
an ancient Pope inside heat to compose
for the lonely

a chill: "Invite yourself into November warmth,"
he might have said, "into the longing that undoes
gloom with smiles." I suppose warmth coats
experience.

Dimensional, epidermic & tame, time makes
chaos into order, yet in a city in November,
the option to leave the café splits
the heat, cold alone.

by Jan King

Mountain View Cemetery

A light rain broke on our walk
undaunted
goldfinches continued their chatter and
Deodars pointed the tips of fingered branches
toward the ground as
the Chinese Elms defied them, widening skyward
to soak their limbs

we trudged on, picking up our pace
against the promise of weightier weather

leash slack, Bosco nosed the ground, on a distinct trail
ahead I caught a movement, weaving
through headstones
stopping among the stillness of stone
a flash of orange/brown appeared, again
Coyote pretended not to see us, lingering
over the scent of a grave

gently, quietly
we turned away, looping
through another part of the cemetery
as we passed the old Farnsworth headstone and
the weeping woman on her eternal pedestal,
I turned
to see coyote had kept pace with us
he locked eyes with mine
stopping, paw
in mid-step

I gathered the leash to me, quickening
our gate and turning away from
the world of his existence on
the periphery of our own, back
to the rain which
dropped like
a curtain

by Cybele Garcia Kohel

On the day of Comey's firing

My son and I
buried
a baby bird

its fragile shell
still protecting
a fledgling form

we dug a hole
where it is sheltered from wind
from storm

cardboard roll as coffin
granite stone marks
the resting spot

this fragile entity perished
when its caretakers
unwilling, or unable to defend it
let it perish

my son and I
made the funerary procession
his soft tears, a eulogy

my hard thoughts
unspoken
against the quiet death
of our country

by Cybele Garcia Kohel

Hospital Haiku

sunlight
over the city
cancer day hospital

trickle of water
in a hospital fountain
fluid infusion

the number of petals
on a daisy
another MRI

embarrassing moment
the nurse acts as if
he's seen it before

left alone
a nurse covers me
with a warmed blanket

curtains between
infusion chairs
how my world has shrunk

whistleblower PET scan

by Deborah P Kolodji

Untitled

together
under the Moreton Bay Fig
autumn light

by Deborah P Kolodji

Untitled

backyard waterfall
the pond brims with mosquito
fish

by Deborah P Kolodji

Lucky

Villanelle for Robin Sean Kraai

The long long months of waiting are over.
At nine pounds and one ounce he has appeared.
Feels as if we've found a four-leaf clover.

He falls asleep on his mother's shoulder.
Her love in his tiny face is mirrored.
The long long months of waiting are over.

He's hungry. His little cries have told her.
To this wiggly bundle, we are endeared.
Feels as if we've found a four-leaf clover.

At Joshua Tree he'll climb a boulder.
His father's kiss is scratchy with his beard.
The long long months of waiting are over.

Time seemed to move along slow and slower.
Into our hearts, cupid's arrow has speared.
Feels as if we've found a four leaf clover.

Celebrate milestones as he gets older.
Anticipation rose, arrival neared.
The long long months of waiting are over.
Feels as if we've found a four-leaf clover.

by Linda Kraai

Published in *Poetic Gestalt*, 2019

A Moment

A moment of peace and contentment
When?

Only after
 all the chores are finished
 the animals fed
 the floors and doors cleaned
 the political news chewed 80 times before swallowed

The choking sensation mid swallow

The overflow of liquid sorrow spilling across
 the sunken cheeks of the the Hungry and Dis-Placed

by Joan Krieger-Hoffman

Dell Av

Dell is an avenue, its bridges arcing over small fish too quick in the water to name. Along the footpaths, out of town guests walk behind their hosts. On either side, doors open into living rooms and kitchens where realtors host open houses. This is how we learn what living here is like.

Mallards float southwest on Howland Canal and northeast on Carroll, diving for small crustaceans, surfacing, diving again. Before we tour the empty houses, we watch them a while. Afterwards, we watch again.

If we lived here we'd watch the paddling and diving day after day.

We fly home wishing we were born into that other life, that rarer life, that life as iridescent as the mallard's green cheek.

> *Eyes wide, the mallard*
> *does not count our shadows*
> *but counts one dark fish.*

by Tom Laichas

Bartholomaus Canyon Renewed

Only your curves were familiar, old friend,
the last time we met.
A red-hot razor had shaved your cheeks
to gray stubble:
only tufts of roasted yucca
and boiled-out elder tree shells
broke through the ash
of your naked hills and gullies.
Fifty years of life destroyed in a day,
one tiny bone on a charred rock
the only memorial of thriving generations
of ground squirrels.

I hear some now:
a syncopated chirping chorus
warning of boots that scuff and stop.
They've dug new homes
under sprawling crops of
bitter, white-trumpeted datura,
dead-headed brittle-bush,
luscious green poison oak,
hardy pink-blossomed mallow,
and invincible castor beans.
California sunflowers flex and show off
against banks of dead, dry mustard stalks,
thistles, and rye grass, product of a wet winter
and—sad to break it to you, old friend—
fuel for your next fire.

Sad only to me.
You've burned and risen, burned and risen,
long before we became neighbors,
long before I learned your features
and collected your dust and foxtails,
long before you learned
my bootprints and the aura of my sweat.

You, who have borne the weight of
sabre-toothed cats and giant ground sloths,
shimmied through eons of grinding tectonic trauma,
and rotated your crops between holocausts,
you value my puny displacement of earth and air
less than that little bone on your oven-black rock,
invisible now under your shaggy new beard.

by Peter Larsen

Chateau Room 57

for Leonard Cohen

it has been two months
since LA has seen the sun
i have gone pale as this room
i have been diffused
the sky reaches into corners
white on white
glances off the service tray
seeps into our lungs
somewhere below open windows
traffic moves over painted arrows
and in the curtains' chilly breath
you can hear Cohen's whisper
i too am a ghost here
haunting the halls of confidence
stealing tea and oranges
to fuel my masterpiece

by Courtney Lavender

green in october

the desert wind heaves into the valley
like clockwork
sidewalks ticking
with the tumble of crackling leaves
in LA we call fall
fire season
we mark seasons by scent
by slant of the sun
in morning you might find a leaf
limp, alone
90 degrees
and green in october

by Courtney Lavender

if my sight goes, i know

on the greyest days
the clouds were paintbrush water
a sweet smudge of sorrow
the memory of colour
at the height of searing summer
when grass was scorched upon the earth
streets shimmered
like rivers
and when she died
the sky - more vivid, vibrant -
held the moon aloft
with a blue that did astound me

by Courtney Lavender

That Afternoon

When the greenest grass shouts "Summer!"
When the wisteria climbs over winter's gray wall
When lilacs breathe out their heavy, enticing scent
When the jacaranda dance in their unique blue gowns
When you and I made bouquets of wild yellow flowers
 To gladden the country mailboxes --
 As much a surprise for someone as Spring
 When the mulberries stained our hands and lips
 To royal purple, and the rosy haze of pollen
 Made us sneeze and sneeze
 And hold each other up

And we laughed and laughed

                    And there was nothing for it but to love

by Nancy Lind

An Affirmation, not a Death Rattle in Bed

"I did a good job!" she says, sitting up - not dead
Her spirit shines through as a warrior for years
Mom battled the dread to know God's blessings
were always true for her, me, you- all of us too

"Please be kind to those 'C' students like me
Give them chances to choose 'Yes' or 'No'
to feel good where ever they may go
Just kept watering the sweet peach tree

Used to go swish-ing in her green taffeta party dress out the door
going with Daddy-o to the Toastmasters' speech floor
Makes her look like the Loretta Young princess once more
I am hand sewin' on her favorite light baby blue soft love skirt
I wore when I was pregnant with first baby Christina

Mom likes comfy clothes for her rest
No make-up needed for her light to shine through
Irene was a natural beauty—oh, so true
Like the angel she was, Irene swept my dad off his feet

Her Confirmation by me in the sun
"Yes, Mom, you did - do a good job!
I love you, Momzie, Irene Julia Hinnen Albright!"

by Janis Lukstein

A version appeared in the *Palos Verdes Library District 2019 Anthology*

Dancing Daffodils

no

O sun-yellow daffodils in full bloom
Give me flowers for every room
Ten thousand for Wordsworth's sake
with golden daffodils from the lake
dancing sprightly 'neath cherry trees
fluttering, light butterflies in the breeze

Tis a memory forever to please . . . .

by Janis Lukstein

The Poetry Corner, The CUB News, Bear Valley Springs, Tehachapi, Ca about 2012.

Morning Coffee

I gently untie myself from my dreams
and slip into the morning
leaving my warmth behind.

Your scent follows me
as I walk from room to room
light scattering across the floor
holding some invisible part of you.

I wait in muffled silence
watching the dog as she nudges the backdoor
wanting to go outside
I ignore her
for now, searching.

I get lost
in the steam that rises
from the cup of coffee
sitting on the counter before me
like an exclamation.

My day ends
before it begins.

by Joseph Lusnia

Honey, She's Gone

"Honey, she's gone".
Hearing preceded sight
For there she was
Still, not cold, no longer struggling for breath.

And I wondered why I had fallen asleep and he hadn't?
And I wondered, "Did she know I'd fallen asleep?"
And in an instant, it didn't matter.

In that instant I was glad she was free.
In that instant I knew we'd need to call the nurse and let Them know.
In that instant I wanted to be held
Hoping the holding would take away the pain of the Future.

We pushed the button and the nurse came in
She saw her and nodded her head, and began to weep as she left the room
They'd known each other from before and there was comfort for me in
her tears.

We sat for a moment and then we wanted to give her body a last bit of care.

Her hands were hints of green veins beneath brown fine skin
Fragile skin covering arthritic hands
That had been altered by time and medication
Delicate skin that had bruised at the slightest touch
Thin skin, still pliant, still mobile.

It was in that moment that I needed to care that the tape not tear at her.
Together we began a task that was our last gift to her body

We carefully held her hand, as we had when it was warm,
And we gently, ever so gently, made sure that tapes
That had been about death approaching
Would be removed with gentleness and love.

We would touch her hands again, but our warmth and her coolness
Would bear witness to Separation of space and time
This last time her hands were still pliant, responding to the
Final time we would hold her hand in love.

by Roberta Martinez

Waltzing in Nepantla

My tongue leaned toward Nepantla.
It did not feel in-between
Instead
It embraced the English, the Spanish, the Nahuatl, the Caló
Like a delicious dessert that I savored
Feeling the vowels and consonants gliding around my teeth;
Leaping from my tongue; painting my thoughts and my ideas.

Nepantla nestled deep in my being
Exploding into pieces that informed my soul;
Washing over my synaptic self
And drew me into deeper questions of
Who I am and where do I belong?
What's mine to claim?
How do I set the limits while I am still learning?
How do I live day to day
In a non-Nepantla World?

My heart chooses not
To walk or march in binomes
Just because my feet
Have been trained to walk in double time.

I will waltz in Nepantla
Because my soul
Will have it no other way.

by Roberta Martinez

Catalyst

Silver leaves trickle
Down the wind
Like so many glass etchings
Belonging to the fragile night

They told me I couldn't write like this
So I stood
With my back to their ignorance
And placed my hand
On the wild wind

by Deborah McGaffey

Previously published in *Rebel Heart*, 2016

The Rim

White Mountains, Arizona, 1987

At the rim
of a canyon
he stands
staring down,
dwarfed by
Ponderosa Pine
and Aspen.
Hands in the pockets
of a pale windbreaker
that rides up in back,
in his polyester pants
and shined dark loafers
my father is a shock
of white hair
and hawk nose
gazing into
a striated throat,
layers and ledges
of sandstone
and granite.
Two feet back
from the edge,
does he see
a future
in a world
that won't

renew itself
in color
for the next
30 years,
does he see
where he'll
step out?

by Penelope Moffet

Water Lilies

*Bad
transmission
poem*

In South Sudan
a woman wades
through water muddied
by the movement of her feet,
collecting water lilies.

Lily roots are hard to eat
says the blonde correspondent
standing nearby,
microphone in hand,
khakis darkened by the swamp.

Plants are held up so we,
the audience at home
half-napping in our chairs,
too full from what we ate,
can see.

The Sudanese woman
barely glances at the camera,
which anyway prefers
the skeletal child
starving in a nearby camp.

We think we are immune.
We think the suffering
flickering in our homes
on nightly news
belongs to others.

Each night driving home
beneath an overpass I see
someone under blankets.
A thin hand lifts
and falls, plucks at cloth.

Someone who
once lived inside
like me.

by Penelope Moffet

Description of My Heart

My heart is a rock
made of lava from a volcano.

My heart is a flame
that burns deep within my soul.

My heart is a star
that shines in the night
that no one can touch.

My heart is a golden locket
buried in a treasure chest
that no one knows about.

Inside my heart there is a little dark room
where I sit on the edge of my bed, alone.

by Andrea Seferina Morales

The Joy and Sadness of Flowers

Hope is a flower
with big white petals
It grows in a rose garden
in your own backyard.

Hurting is a flower
that grows among bricks
that trip you.
It has a trap
that springs shut
and it eats bugs.

Sadness is four black flowers
in a dark cemetery
at midnight
when it's cold and misty.

Laughter is a bouquet
of carnations,
pink, red, and white,
that fall out of the sky
as you run across
a grassy meadow
with your little kitten.

by Andrea Seferina Morales

For My Mom

To my Mom
who always
keeps the house clean
To my Mom
who plays piano
in the garage
Who once in a blue moon
calls me mija
To my Mom
who brings me presents
when I least expect it
To my Mom who I love -
If I were a tree
You would be the dove
that sings in my branches.

by Andrea Seferina Morales

A Little Taste of Wine

My golden retriever—
Jethro is his name—
never ceases to wag his tail
he drinks wine
Chardonnay or Merlot
red or white he laps it up
he drinks wine
because of my guilt
I never take him for a walk
or make him fetch a ball
I don't have time for my dog.

My golden retriever
when I'm home
he's always at my side
never tries to run away
even when I leave
the door wide open
he stays right by my side
my dog drinks wine
and stinks because
I don't bathe him.

My golden retriever Jethro,
he doesn't eat because
I forget to buy him food
but he never fails to
drink the Tokay
the last time

I remembered
to take him
to the veterinarian
to avoid a fine
I gave him the works
the shots he needed
a bath and flea dip
an anal squeeze
a buzz cut
it cost a fortune.

My dog Jethro
the golden retriever
wags his tail
eager to go home
to drink wine
to celebrate
we both decided
never to go back
that dog care
takes too much away
from my dog
the golden retriever's
wine-drinking money.

I have to clean up after him
all over the house
even the cleaning lady
she doesn't come any more
nobody visits us
I'm the only one
who cares for him

it's my fault
because of my guilt
I pour Jethro
a big bowl of Tokay
he's losing weight
he's losing hair
he even shakes
he still wags his tail
ever so slowly
he wags his tail
excited when he accompanies me
with a little taste of wine

by Alejandro Zapote Morales

Eminent Domain

Eminent domain was the word
used to frighten and steal land
from young and old survivors of
El Sueño where babies play at
the feet of one-hundred-year-old
storytellers who foretold that
la gente were going to lose their
jacales and valued land after the
coming of the *políticos*
who walked the dusty
paths caressed the rich soil
discovered the economically
 physically vulnerable
"¡pueblo mexicano!"

Who lived in El Sueño
an instant to a lifetime
a lifetime to an instant
those wise men and women
who years ago were
paracaidistas whom
the government let stay
on faraway worthless land
forgotten and now discovered
by the politicos del Palacio Naciónal
who visited waving eminent domain
to pilfer land from the good citizenry

Old and young built houses that
endured floods earthquakes fire
drought, and family feuds still
the houses cobijan la estirpe
who knead the soil everyday
a struggle for la tortilla
there in that place *buenos mexicanos*
stay to guard their turf and
toil with life's pleasures and agonies

In their domain
a small house
a small lot
a small street
where ignored history resides

There some years ago
someone took a photograph
of a number of happy families
standing before a *milpa*
their many children sat at their feet
playing with golden ears
of corn piled in front

The photograph fell in the hands of
a presidential assistant who thought
ideal *para la compañía canadense*
and sent UNAM engineers with
magic tools to measure
the land for a factory
like feet for *guaraches*

The dwellers of El Sueño
did not need guaraches
no matter how shiny the colorful beads
that decorated the brown leather
did not need a factory

by Alejandro Zapote Morales

Self-Defense

1

Carrying a 3-inch knife—
raped earlier that morning
argued with her mother
the petite woman ran out of the apartment
hysterical and confused
she wandered through streets mourning

2

the cops come
to serve and protect
the woman
all of 19 years
stood still
to return
a desperate gaze
at two police officers
a glimpse of help
a glimmer of hope

3

Drop the knife!
Drop the knife!
the officers yell in unison
as they advance toward her
Drop the knife!

She stumbles forward

4

Neighbors mill, rage and shout:
use your batons! they scream at the cops.
bring her down a different way!
It's 2 of you, you can jump on her!
Look at her, look at her!
she is beyond scared and disoriented!

Neighbors screamed as bullets flew:
the knife the knife!
it's just a little knife!
knock it out of her hand!
use a baton, a rifle butt, a kick!

6

Neighbors screamed and cried,
Forming a half moon in the street:
let us overwhelm her
and make her give up the knife!
Let the neighbor women
smother the girl in their garments and love
to save her life!
the knife is not a threat!

7

the first shots
fired in unison

pierced her shoulders and arms
the repeated volleys
penetrate her chest
Drop the knife!
she is still standing

the department's bullets
ripped her upper torso to shreds
knocked her backward
till she rests on the lawn
body sprawled opened wide
crucified in a growing
pool of blood

8

19 years old
shot 35 times
at 7 in the morning
by 2 cops trained to
shoot to kill
and not much more

by Alejandro Zapote Morales

Weather

Yesterday.
Sun-filled
Warm
and
Peaceful.
The old Ash tree
standing in front
of the
little red farmhouse
continues to
rain leaves.
The blazing inferno
now extinguished.
The sky
no longer smokey
is blue again.
Swallows are back.
Songs fill the air.
This morning.
cool, cloudy and sunless.
Feels like rain
and
I
want to dance.

by Toni Mosley

And the Last Shall Be Earth

The garden hose stretches, soaking an orange
lifting its laden arms from the Earth.

Temperate morning, eggshell of blue,
green life, the Goldilocks charm of the Earth.

I get up at six, shower, have tea, loft
a wisp in the blanket warming the Earth.

I want light, food, ice, heat, art, plastics, screens
but do not mean any harm to the Earth.

I wept, when I read of species' deaths,
over what my own car meant for Earth

and walked to the store, a round trip two miles,
underfoot seeking the *dharma* of Earth.

Each birth is sacred, mysterious, sweet
but all together we swarm on the Earth,

mine, burn it, plow it, an Anthropocene,
busily making a farm of the Earth.

Drought. Fire. Break glass! Hurricane. Flood.
Panicked, we sound an alarm for the Earth

and plan for flight on the tarmac, from Earth.
Soul, press this one life to dark fragrant earth.

by Janet Nippell

Back When I Rode the Bus

Back when I rode the bus things were simple.
I didn't have to ride it, won't lie.
I cared for Earth, I enjoyed people.

Looking up downtown, at my stop on schedule,
big window framing a pink morning sky—
back when I rode the bus things were simple.

To tug the yellow cord, the looping bell-pull,
unless someone tugged it first, feeling that tie,
caring for Earth, enjoying people,

made our shared ride a church without steeple.
No one knew how fast the water would rise.
Back when I rode the bus things were simple.

Bus-riding now won't stop the debacle.
Bent over mobile phones, prodding thumbs fly.
We don't cool Earth, I fear for people

but pay the odd fare on principle.
Mostly I'm down with the cars grinding by.
Back when I rode the bus things were simple.
Earth-care came easy and joy in people.

by Janet Nippell

Ether

There is a silence calling me
Too familiar, and yet unknown.
Like the untold lives of we, overburdened with stagnation.
And though I fear in wake of the world before me
I recognize its impermanence.
Blindly traveling like a celestial body
Seeking to become part of a collective entity.
My solemn wish is
That I be diluted

by Christian Nuno

Untitled

I'm killing myself
With a stress-full mind
That needs to provide
A world
Where I belong as an ally
To my own conscious.
Unable to ignore the fact that I'm
Trying to exist in a world
So much bigger than myself
I'd much rather dissipate
Into a cosmos
Where I could belong everywhere.
It's hurting me.
And I'm definitely dying
to get to the next infinity

by Christian Nuno

Impractical

We simply want someone to care about the things we do.
In all this fantastic mundane glory, so our time here does not in fact feel
disposable.
What is the use of even writing this?
I could spend my time outside
building a kite,
despite
the
rain.

by Christian Nuno

Dandelions

I received good grades in math because I solved
the problems. My answers were the right answers.

I received poor grades in life because I caused
the problems. My actions were the wrong actions.

The dandelion loses itself through the forces of nature,
emerging again at the landing places of seedlings,

withering, its life spent, parting without dignity, the crumpled
remnants of sun-drenched glory, soon to be no more.

I have seen my mother lose herself like the dandelion.
Her crumpling is not a math problem to be solved.

No right answers.

I write this poem, but I am not good enough as a poet.
To work on skills does little good. I need this poem today.

As seedlings float in the air, memories of life with Mom
emerge again in different landscapes and terrains,

persisting despite frailty, in family memories, musical
melodies, personal traits, values, which last forevermore.

by Dean Okamura

Staying between the lines

I remember learning how to drive a car.
Excitement surged within me when
I pressed down on the accelerator.
All that horsepower at my control.
My new responsibility.
To drive on the highway was quite a change
from being a small kid in the back seat
going along for the ride.
The driver's training instructor said
to point the car off into the distance.
This was the way to stay between the lines.
Others said to match a part of the car
with the left line was the proper technique.
I remember bringing you home from the hospital.
All those techniques I learned in the parenting classes.
My new responsibility was quite a change
from being a young child. One who thought little about
what it meant to be an adult.
Never considering
what it meant to be a parent.
Would I stay within the parenting lanes?
Raise you right?
Now you're grown up.
An adult.
How the years passed by!
I dropped you off at the airport.
You are traveling for work.
We did all right.
Didn't we?

I let go of the wheel.
Let you drive yourself.
And off you went,
staying between the lines.

by Dean Okamura

inner/outer

Kindle that youthful fire
don't let the love die out

When we start to fear love
the embers turn to ash

The cold comes closer the older we get
Keep dancing with the flames
Keep hearing laughter from the cracks
Our youthful fire will always dance back

by Atlakatl Orozco

Te Quiero Decir

Te quiero decir, que te amo.
Desde la primera vez que yo te vi.
Queria conocerte,
Y por eso te sigue.
No estaba preocupado,
De donde vamos a llegar.
Porque siempre lo sentía,
Que tu serias mi hogar.
Pero tambien te deje ir,
Para que vives tu vida.
Siempre pensando en ti,
Mientras que yo vivo la mía.
Esperando para el momento perfecto,
Para hacerte mía.
Esperando, para verte otra vez
Contarte Todas las cosas que yo aguanto,
Todo en mi corazón.
Viendo te levanta mi alma.
Imagino todo lo que podemos hacer.
Ausencia de ti me duele,
No pensaba dejarte sola,
Evitando un amor sincero.
Y cuando lo sientes, mi amor, vas a saber que
Yo siempre te voy a querer.

by Kelving Ortiz

Published 09/24/19 by *Intercultural Press*

I Want to Tell You

I want to tell you, I love you,
Since the first time I saw you.
I wanted to meet you,
And so I followed you.
I wasn't worried
Where we'd arrive
Because I've always felt it,
That you would be my home.
But I also let you go,
For you to live your life.
Always thinking of you,
While I live mine.
Waiting for the perfect moment,
To make you mine.
Waiting to see you again,
Tell you all the stories,
All the things that I endure,
Everything in my heart.
Viewing you lifts my soul
I imagine everything we could do.
Absence of you hurts me.
Never would I think to leave you alone,
Evading a sincere love. And when
You feel it, my love,
You'll know that I will always love
You.

By Kelving Ortiz

(Te Quiero Decir-English Translation) 03/18/20

Pantuom with Cuban Street Poets

How are you it's been a while
Can you spare some time
I really miss your smile
No I'm not okay but I think I'm doing fine

Can you spare some time
I know It's hard to get together
No Im not okay but I think I'm doing fine
I appreciate the effort

I know It's hard to get together
Everybodys gotta work
I appreciate the effort
Just know it kinda hurts

Everybodys gotta work
And I just got this song
Just know it kinda hurts
You didn't hear it now you're gone

And I just got this song
I really miss your smile
You didn't hear it now you're gone
How are you it's been a while

by Luis Ortiz

Revolutionary Seeds

Yo Soy Xicanx Indígena.
I say this honoring the skulls that have come before mine–
the blood they shed for me to breathe in the dark.

Yo soy Xicanx Indígena.
And you can't take that from me.

Yo soy Xicanx Indígena.
Histories forever intertwined,
That neither you or I could tear apart.

Yo soy Xicanx Indigena.
Mestizaje? Mixed-blood?
Ni de aqui, Ni de alla,
But we are here–
and we are screaming,
We exist to resist.

Soy Xicanx Indígena.
Fuck your boxes and forms–
That leave out my identity.

Soy Xicanx Indígena.
Tomas tus licuados but you can't stand the taste
Of mixed-raices in your mouth.

Soy Xicanx Indígena.
Esquites, Milpa, Hot Cheetos & Cheese.

Soy Xicanx Indígena.
Blood Maid de Maiz;
My skin holds ancient Maya secrets-
that my Spanish grandfathers have kept from me.

Soy Xicanx Indígena.
This spirit is greater than me,
Greater than us,
Yet it is all I know,
To bring me back home-
La Tierra.

Soy Xicanx Indígena.
You can take the cihuatl out of Maravilla,
But you can't take the Maravilla out of me.

Yo soy Xicana Indígena.
Mujersita Zapatista
Lost en el encuentro,
But the path has found me.
El camino de sangre rojo.

by Mixchel Payan

Milk and Hyacinth

My first class was taught by a man,
a little clingy in cottons and sneakers,
the salt scent of the asanas, quiet.

Today my teacher's voice
is jeweled and winnowed,
a palimpsest.

She strides like flying,
with the grace of an Echo Park dove,
aiming, calling softly, slowing hearts.

Sure weather, her voice
in petals, rhythm, history.
With her gravity works well.

To mirror, to keep right from left
she describes milk and hyacinth,
Tadasana, Trikonasana.

She aids our breath,
our speed, our strength,
she leaves none behind.

With her this day, this class, these moments,
I witness the shifting down of time,
the moving of an age, the perfection of us.

A practice of body magic
since before she could sit.
She is she and not of me.

She in yoga grace
is my daughter,
Miranda,
my child.
My master.

by Bill Ratner

Locker Room Talk

Hidden in succulents beneath my window,
a machete, a chainsaw.
My shoulders hulk with ripsaw dust,
my brow, my throat.

I am an unreliable,
a bulky, squatting mannequin
with gum pink lips.

I freeway my hair with orange blossoms,
listen to the cry of chachalacas,
the great kiskadee, dharma talk.
I have to try.

My friends look like Lauren Bacall.
I introduce them as Dave.
I am out of cigarettes,
ruby, bloodshot, blind.

We are barely alert to the emergency,
a din of piercing dread
no longer distant.

Wrenched out of torpor,
bodies sprint toward
the scene of the crime
just down the street.

Hate restarts.
Masters of Horror.
Reptilian mind.
Trump.

Will I sign on with others to seek redress?
Will I celebrate violence?
I keep thinking I have a killer punch.
What if I miss?

by Bill Ratner

Balms

"When we pivot ... to the blade of grass, the note
of music, the line of a novel, ... we breathe
and are revived."
—Ava Du Vernay

Each place I sit, and take a breath
to catch a break from life,
simple gifts from earth, ocean, sky,
from gods and goddesses of all that is not man,
suffuse me with their balm.

On my patio, on tables under gingko trees,
in backyard bowers of jasmine and pine,
in cottage rooms darkened with dusk
or lit by morning sun,
gifts I've gathered soothe my grateful eyes:

> Stones rounded smooth like eggs, roosting
> serene in bowls and nests fashioned by hand.

> Rocks shaped like hearts, adopted from creek
> beds, forests, deserts when I take our dog around.

> Shells iridescent, fragile, crescent, large like
> helmets, or conches furled unto themselves.

> Bamboo platters piled with sand and bits of
> wood the waves spat up.

Pine cones nestled in orange rinds, their
fragrance intertwined.

Petals sprinkled across tablecloths with
beeswax candles and pedestals of pears.

I waft from room through room,
from garden to patio and back,
bits of nature greeting me at every turn,
to calm, to keep me grounded to the dust,
to sands, wind and sun, trees and rocks,

to keep me grounded
to the mighty and the small,
to all that we've been and will be again—
to keep me grounded to
the simple and the simply grand.

by Thelma T. Reyna

Like a Politician, No Tears

...my friend told me when the memorial ended, with a sidewise
glance at my face as I stepped on clods and burrs on the narrow
cemetery path wending my way to my husband's open grave. "It
was amazing," he blurted. "In your entire speech, not one tear. Like
a politician!"

But yes there were tears. I smiled through them and he was fooled.
I spoke softly to solemn faces and there were tears. I recounted my
husband's pain and there were tears. My friend, too far back, was
fooled by calm.

For three days when my husband died, I cried ducts dry, endured
stone throat that swallowed speech. Paths of sun and moon
entwined till light and dark.

The paper of my speech was mottled and edges curled with
wetness.

blank face, lips moving
—for they must, they must say words—
heart beating limply

       broken hearts dissolve
      the same in rain or sunbeams
        ...quiet, loud, unparsed

by Thelma T. Reyna

Convalescent Hospital

...for my husband

You were in the convalescent, fourth month, the only
smiling face amongst four patients lined like bowling pins
in skinny metal beds, pinned like pins in cotton coverlets,
contained, wood visages facing swinging door that
swooshed and closed for trays, needles, pills, gauze, and
 all that kept your fellows' faces glum, eyes glazed.

Yesterday you slipped from bed, landed on linoleum dust,
so now they've placed a gel pad at the edge where
slippers hit when you pull yourself upright with knuckles
curled on your walker. Now they watch like hawks, the
star of the alley now, your name in black sharpie
scrawled on caution signs pinned to your bed and walls.

You're always the star: shoulders slooped, buttocks slack,
arm drooping when you sit, glasses smudged with butter
from breakfast biscuits but who cares. Halogen examination
lamps don't out-watt your hopeful eyes. Weary fingers take
your pulse, turn you this way, that, change soiled gowns,
but can't dim the stars that illuminate your smile.

Three dessicated men lined like wood beside you, dozing,
headphones blurring snores, eyes nailed to Fox or HBO,
eyes divorced from wives, sisters, brothers who ceased
pilgrimage to these bedsides months ago. But you, you're
the star unswallowed by black holes, the star unblocked
by eclipses part or whole, starlight blooming undeterred.

by Thelma T. Reyna

Our love (though Jhene Aiko song titles)

Nobody gave me a warming
There was no sign
We started as **Strangers**
We began to explore each other's lives
Making connects through past **Pain**
Frequency radiates between us now
We had no idea what was in store for us next
Brave souls lead us to become more
That more led us to not **Wait no More**
You weren't mine
And I not yours
All I know is you always made me **Feel Like a Man**
We made **Promises** to each other we couldn't keep
Leading us on this **Bad Trip**
Lost in **Oblivion**
It's Cool though
Only **When We Love** each other
Those days brought a **New Balance**
That I soon realized would be **Moments** only found in my memory of you
I'd Rather Be with no one else
But **the pressures** began to be too much once again
We went to escape in the clouds
We got higher and **higher**
Now **The Worst** has come
Addiction
Now it's **You vs Them**
The demons that embody you as we reach for the exit
We continue down this pass until we **Won't Play the Game** any more
The **Ways** of this relationship is unhealthy

An **Angel** had appeared
In the shape of therapy and sober living
Now separated
 I can see the toxins we bring
Spotless Mind brings clarity and understanding
We were never meant to be
No matter what
I
Will
Always
Love
You

by Joshua Rodgers

I am queer poetry

I
As in singular
As in me
Meaning the stories told are though my eyes
The shoes I walk in
Lives that have affected me

Queer
A label
Box
Trending on
Twitter
Tumbler
Instagram
The talk of the town
Even still people hide
Enough to include but keep separate
A new way of operation in society
The sashay of my mister sister as she twists at the ball
The calls of queens
Reclaimed empowerment of something once derogatory

Poetry
An idea
Manifested into artistry
Ability to shape society
Agenda with a purpose
Creative
Free

Melodies of the heart sang in a cappella
Hymns of my ancestors
The swing of the hips of my sister as she beckons a potential mate
Response to the chaos in the world to create a beautiful masterpiece of change
Existence of blackness
I am queer poetry

by Joshua Rodgers

Grandfather's Ring

Kicking off your shoes you ran laughing to the water's end.
Trailing paths of sand and shells, I followed.
At first touch the ocean circled around our hands.
Your eyes were amethyst flecked with gold.
My ring was violet in the April air.

I lost my ring in the water
where for a moment I could see it—
glinting like a purple star.
Then the water took it. You told me
I'd always know exactly where it was;
but nothing stays just where it falls.

Now several April's since, you are gone,
the ring and the while space it left on my hand.
I see oceans too circle back to touch the shore.

Today, in the too-cold shallows I glimpsed
a piece of abalone shell, petal-shaped, white,
with a rim of purple scalloped round
like the slender lash of an eye. I reached for it
through water so clear I could almost see my smile,
and missing only shell, grasped everything.

by Susan Rogers

Grateful Conversations: A Poetry Anthology, 2018

Longing for October

I looked for you
among leaves
so full of color

they burst
like cherry flames
singing of sap.

I looked for you
in the blood of autumn—
trees warmed by sunfire

spinning in the pulse
of maple and beech
anthocyanin sugaring

green veins
as spring sugars
the sky with sakura.

I looked for you
in the chill of autumn,
mountains filling

the sweep of space
with strokes of brilliance
knowing it is both

fire and frost
that paints the tree,
knowing every love

turns to deeper shades
of longing as it rises
into fullness.

You are wind
and water moving
across the face of leaves.

You are the invisible
made visible,
sap rising

until it explodes
in a symphony of light
everywhere I look

in the canopy.

by Susan Rogers

Sunflowers in Your Hand

for Jane

I wonder if I will recognize you
when you return
in a different form.
I like to think your breath
so intimately part of mine
that when you are reborn
even if you wear
white organza as a bride,
or the black habit of a nun,
if you appear much younger
than you were
in a sweater striped in cyan blue
with wild sunflowers in your hand
I will remember you,
just as I remember the shine
of a sun dazzled stream
after it's gone dry, the rhythm
of staccato rain when I swing
my hammock under cloudless skies.
Or the sound of laughter
in a dream of exquisite joy.
Even if you choose to be my cat,
a hummingbird, a bright scaled koi.
And If you are born in another country,
don't speak words I understand
if you are not female this time
but instead a boy, I hope there will be

some note of you that sings,
your music indisputably
through the differences of then and now,
so I will know you are the one
that it's you come back
in whatever form you come.

by Susan Rogers

Quill and Parchment, 2019

Momento Mori for Petit Mort

Guttural sensation
speaks tactually,
like fingers digging
into handbag's contents,
searching for lost keys;
or like tender touch
explored by lovers
seeking ecstasy's reach.

Somewhere underneath tough
skin, supple points of
intersection meet,
awaiting those who seek
to discover sweet,
secreted places,
reserved by the meek,
for just one person's peek.

Yet, aft' flesh is buried,
only tombstone's words
speak to intimate
sweet nothings' whispering,
that touched another
with privacy's breach,
momentarily
captured, timelessly.

by Michael Romero

Secondary Inspections: A Sestina

✓ of at the least the real part

3 minutes

A nose, a foreign look, a memory. "They just want to know if you are Jewish,"
your mom says of questions about what country you came from;
you know that you'll never pass for who you are. Everyone foreign claims your face.
City of Angels swelters, everyone here from somewhere else, still they ask,
"Where were you born?" and "How do you say 'Hello'?" You answer fearing hatred.
Fear you came by naturally after strip search and secondary inspections. Not beautiful.

"Go to New York—you'll be sought out" the statuesque, unapologetically beautiful
Black, Columbian woman says. Not here, you're Toucan Sam, you're a Jew.
"Angelenos look for an airbrushed effect, images of themselves," she says. Hatred
for your ancestral look. "You have only a slight accent, where are you from?"
Later old Armenian men shout out greetings from their balconies, ask
questions you can't understand. You only know your strong nose on face

too ugly for years. For a girl. And you're hairy. White Angelenos seek their own face,
lips full, not too ethnic, unless ambiguous, not too angular, no rough edges. Beautiful.
Customs guards interrogate, hands grab your body. In Greece, Danish boys ask
you for towels, assume you are from Parros. Jewish
journalist writes story, gets tweets – his beheaded caricature rises from
desire to make America white again. You are zoo animals watched by hatred.

You fear reaction to your ancestral aura. You find hidden outposts of hatred.
City of Angels where everyone came from somewhere else. Yet your face
looks foreign. Daily you hear, "no where are you really from?"
No use saying you are second generation born in America, land of the beautiful.
Your mom's answer to that was always, "They only want to know if you're Jewish."
You go with your son on a field trip, "What tribe are you?" Cherokee guide asks.

"Of course we both came across the Bering Straits." he says and doesn't ask
"where are you really from?" when you answer. Shows no hatred.
"From Russia, Hungary, Palestine, Turkey," you say and tell him you're Jewish.
Watch what hashtag you use, lest it shows up as a cross burned on your Facebook
page. Maybe it's true what the Columbiana says, "Go to New York, you'd be beautiful
there." Here, your Black son looks like someone they might shoot or run from.

You look like someone might be rounded up, asked "where from?"
A man lingering outside 7-11, looks at you both and asks,
"Egyptian?" Your son mimes the walk like Egyptian dance, your beautiful
son. Later he says, "I guess there's more racism than I thought," hatred
spewing out of a parking attendants mouth spits as he yells at a face
that looked a lot like my son. KKK leader posts "Of course they're not white. Jews."

You're looked upon with suspicion, hatred, wondering where you're from
Will they look at our faces, hear an unspoken word and ask?
You wonder: In New York, will I be beautiful, will we be safe? Jew and Afro-Jew.

by Carla Sameth

Previously published: *Unlikely Stories*, Mark V. March 9, 2018

I Didn't Ask to be Mexican

When the Creator *Ipalnemohuani Ometeotl*
sent me from the stars to earth,
I didn't ask to be Mexican,
I just got lucky.
I didn't ask to be the hummingbird's friend
or creator of high civilization.
To be the greatest farmer of the world,
or the inventor of zero,
I just got lucky.
Because mis abuelitos, mis abuelitas,
mis nanas, mis tatas
eran *Nahua, catca Maya/Zapoteco/Mexica*, were Mexicans.
Hard working, caring
genius *nanas* de *Anahuac,*
courageous *tatas* de *Cuitlahuac.*
Loving and sharing.
Have you eaten mijo? Ya comistes mija?
Today, tomorrow, again and again,
I didn't ask to be Mexican.
I didn't ask to be the child of a beautiful dark, brown
obsidian eyed mujer.
I just got lucky.
I didn't ask to understand precession,
And how the sky moves 1 degree to the western
direction every 72 years.
Didn't ask for the connection to *Teotihuacan,*
or *Monte Alban,*
to have constructed La Gran *Tenochtitlan*
I just got lucky.

I didn't ask to be a master mason,
a flower arranger or *Bonampak* mural painter.
I never asked for the recipes to tamales or guacamole,
didn't ask for the *chocolate* for the simmering mole.
I just got lucky.
I didn't ask to be an eagle or jaguar
of *Xochicalco* or *Mitla*
to love the hottest chiles,
Quetzalcoatl, Nahuatl, Teocintli.
Nor did I ask to be one of *Tonantzin's* sons,
one of the Turquoise prince's precious ones,
or to have a grand legacy of flowers and songs.
I just got lucky.

by Tony Sandoval

Hummingbird Chant

Nahuatl pronunciation:

"-**Que**-" at the beginning, ending or within a word sounds like "**keh**,"
"-**Qui**-" within a word sounds like "**kee**."
"**Cui**-" within a word is pronounced "**kwee**;"
however, "-**cue**-" would be pronounced "**kweh**"
and "-**cua**-" or "**qua**-" has a "**kwah**" sound.
Furthermore, "**x**" sounds like "**sh**" in English.
"**Ç**" (ç) or "**z**" possesses an "**s**" sound. **i.e.** "ça"is pronounced "**sah**."
"**Hua**-" is pronounced "**wah**," and "-**hue**-" sounds like "**weh**."
"**Hui**" sounds like "**wee**."
Double "**ll**" within a word does not sound like "**y**" as it does in Spanish.
Thus, *calli* is pronounced "**kal-lee**."
A"-**tl**" at end of word such as "**Quetzalcoatl**," the "**l**" is nearly silent.
An "**i**" will sound like "**ih**" or an "**eeeh**" sound.
An "**˜**" symbol over a letter, in most cases, requires a following "**n**" for clarity.
A "**y**" used as a possessive prefix would have an "**i**" or "**ih**" sound.
But it can also have another sound as in *yollotl*, expressed as "**yoh-loht**."
Stress is on the second to last syllable.

"Hummingbird Chant:"

Huitzitzilin tla xihualla	Hummingbird please come.	Colibrí ven por favor.
in xochimeh nimitzmacaz	I will give you flowers	Te daré flores y
in tlahtolli teoxihuitl	and divine turquoise words.	palabras divinas de turquesa.
tototzintli nimitznequi	Oh little bird, I love you.	O pajarito te quiero.

o o ilili aya
o ilili ohuaya

o ilili aya
o ilili ohuaya

Ninoyollo papahpaqui	My heart is so happy	Mi Corazon esta tan contento
cualtipehua tipatlani	when you're about to fly.	cuando está a punto a volar.
xiconana in xochimeh	Take these flowers to the	Lleve estas flores a lugar
campa tehuatl tipahpaqui	place where your most happy.	donde estes más feliz.

o o ilili aya
o ilili ohuaya
o ilili aya
o ilili ohuaya

by Tony Sandoval

Rotation

She heats oil
Rolls puri
Drops flat flour into bubbling oil

> *You conquer*
> > *enforce rules*
> > *ban travel*

In another pan
She pops coriander seeds
Tosses sliced potatoes

> *You build walls*
> > *deport passengers*
> > *obstruct asylum-seekers*

She serves flaky puri
With crisp potatoes
—we devour together

> *You demand documents*
> > *collect fingerprints*
> > *require face-identification*

Our choice: eat, speak, wear
Practice as we please
Where we wish

You cannot hinder climbs
        prevent tide
        stop earth rotation

Like waves we cross
We fly
We roar
We stay or leave
—our movement permanent.

by Sehba Sarwar

Papercuts Magazine Volume 20, Nomad - Fall Issue. <http://desiwriter-slounge.net/articles/papercuts-nomad-sehba-sarwar/>

Justice

Be careful of that word
Remember that saying "yes" to something
means saying "no" to something else.
If ok, then go for it.

If not, then weigh the consequences
and consider them thoughtfully.
Occasionally, they may not be right.
We need to look more closely.

Many injustices have been around for years,
for a very long time.
Does that make them right? Or just what we're used to?
Time to right the wrongs.

Time to say "oh I am used to that
and found a way to ignore them."
But it was an affront to human dignity,
a thoughtless comment, a downright snub.

How did we ever live through that?
How did we ever overcome the second-class feeling?
Oh, yeah, we knew that we were worthwhile
and that God loves us. We knew that.

by Elsa Seifert

Resistance

Resistance is Futile.
Words on the rear window
of the car in front of me
called out my response, "No! It is not!"

I thought about the owner,
exhausted from efforts to resist,
or collapsing in the onslaught
of counter-resistance,

accepting the horror of war, of inequity,
of torture, of loss of freedom,
of exclusion, of the "low IQ"
from consideration of the truth.

I thought of the alternative: One voice, raised in opposition.
One voice magnified in another, yet another voice,
into a cacophony of voices, not ignored.
A movement begins.

by Elsa Seifert

Six

for Officer Darren Wilson who shot
Michael Brown, Ferguson, MO   Aug., 9, 2013

ppsshoommmm! One.
How was it, Officer,
that first pull after his hands raised skyward
gunless and brown?
your lips licking the scent of power
adrenals screaming for a fix

ppsshoommm! Two.
Where in your body did you feel the fear?
groin or the bulls eye
ingrained on your mind's eye?

ppsshoommm! Three.
Hand shaking yet, Wilson?
Will it be better with your woman tonight
now that you've fired the big gun?

ppsshoommm! Four.
are you and your god both
scanning the manual ?
Reasonable force justifiable homicide
Justifiable homicide reasonable force
bloodied mantras for redemption

ppsshoommm! Five.
How many dead men must you kill

232

for the hunter's trophy
stained high fives from the boys in the club?

ppsshoommm! Six.
this self defense against Blackness
six and sixteen, sixty-six, 360
all the Michael Browns are yours now, Darren
a retinue of riddled spirits
hovering til life claims you
without taking a shot.

Nov. 2014

by S. Pearl Sharp

previously published on *Documenting Ferguson (website)*

Sequoia/Cathedral Tree

Vesper service celebration
In a ceiling-less, burned-out tree,
Open skylight to the heavens;
Early evening above is all I see.

I feel like a cub in a den,
Held secure by unseen forces.
I exit with deep gratitude;
Ahead of me lie untrodden courses.

didn't hear first

Awareness is startled awake;
Nearby lies a thick carpet of green.
In treetops grow fresh emerald fronds,
Lush as a leprechaun's dream.

I push to the edge on a ledge;
Hanging Rock makes me feel faint.
Moro Rock glistens in the distance;
I hear singing of forest saints.

I descend and sit on a log;
A limb crashes; birds are disturbed.
Above, night's first star is twinkling;
Profound stillness.

by Pamela Shea

Wolverton Creek

Surging liquid white mane
Of an albino lioness
Cascades over granite,
Imparting courage
And valor.

Below, a cat's eye,
Embedded on ruddy stone,
Gazes downstream
With determination
And confidence.

Mountains echo,
A soft, mellow meowing,
Both comforting
And challenging,
Beckoning.

Heading upstream,
A face watches from tree bark;
Reflections merge
In a quiet pool,
Beaming skyward.

by Pamela Shea

Garden Party

A cosmic picnic
Spreads over patterned cloth

Old themes repeat
As fresh sunrise glistens

Predictability comforts
As the unknown beckons

by Pamela Shea

A Perfect Picture

the rosebush
one branch growing through
the arms of the *nopales*
thorn and quill
budding cactus bright pink against dark green
I hold my breath and gaze
helpless without a camera

by Nancy Shiffrin

Furious is the Night!

Furious is the night!
Moon hides behind
a veil of clouds
too ashamed by
what's going on below...

Tweets and whispers
in high places...
>   *"Go back to where you*
>   *came from..."*

>   North, west, south and east,
>   in big cities and small towns,
>   in stadiums, schools and stores,
>   in bars, cafes and street corners
>   adults, teens, and children chant...
>   >   *"Go back to where you*
>   >   *came from..."*

>   Sound travels -
>   even the trees
>   hear echoes from the past,
>   even the stars weep
>   at such hateful words...
>   >   *"Go back to where you*
>   >   *came from..."*
>   >   *"You don't belong here!"*

Furious is the night!
Furious is the night!

by Dorothy Skiles

Morning Prayers

Every morning
after breakfast,
before exercises,
I pray for strength –

> I cup my hand
> over my right
> knee and spread
> my fingers.
>
> My lips whisper
> a prayer…
> "Heal thy self."
> Mind quiet.
>
> My body listens well,
> tuned to its inner voice,
> to its inner healing
> unseen by my eyes.
>
> With every groan
> from my lips,
> with every stretch,
> pull, tug of the knee,
>
> leg gets stronger,
> knee bends easier
> and I'm on my way to
> leaving the walker behind!

by Dorothy Skiles

Meditation on Divine Names, Moonrise Press 2012, editor Maja Trochimczyk

The Soul of America

The soul of America is steeped in polarities.
Diversity is our normalcy.
We were never a nation of homogeneity:

> North and south
> East and west
> City and rural

Shall I go on?

> Citizens and immigrants
> Migrants and residents
> Indigenous and foreigners

Shall I go on?

> Cubans and Mexicans
> Japanese and Chinese
> Irish and Italians

Shall I go on?

> Christianity and Islam
> Mormon and Judaism
> Buddhism and Hinduism

Shall I go on?

> Democratic and Republican
> Progressive and Conservative
> Independent and Libertarian

Shall I go on?

Our polarities are our commonality.
Our differences are the norm.

So, why do we fear?
Or fight?
Or hate?
Or harm one another?
Our skin colors and countries of origin are not the enemy.
We are all just yearning for the same human needs:

> Warmth....
> Love....
> Compassion...
> Understanding...

by Beverly Tate

Who's Deceiving Whom?

Is it the dark colors of our skins?
Or is it the colors of your uniforms
that conjure chilling images of bodies black and blue?

Who's deceiving whom?
When you juxtapose your feelings of fear with
chilling visuals of black and blue uniformed men:

> Clubbing Rodney...
> Choking Eric...
> Chasing Walker...

Who's deceiving whom?
When black and brown men and women have died
yielding to your black and blue commands:

> Hands up...
> Eyes down...
> Head bowed...
> Bodies supine on the ground...

Who's deceiving whom?
When your past indiscretions precede the
flashing lights of your Black and White:

> Chasing innocent men and women...
> Tracking little children...
> Carrying entire families to jail...

Who's deceiving whom of seeing black and blue?

by Beverly Tate

What Lies Beneath Big Bear Lake

No brown ones or grizzlies,
but my cell phone which leapt out of my pocket
like a flying fish,
sinking my conversations,
my text messages,
and my selfies
down to the dark silt.

The young man I paid to don a wet suit
resurfaced with nothing, not even
my hat which blew straight away one day
upon acceleration,
or my check book and pen
to write upon its soggy pages,
or last summer's half-read book.

He reported seeing
several drain plugs
plastic bottles and straws
now available only upon request,
numerous boats,
several screwdrivers of various sizes,
coins, totes,
and a forest
of fish hooks and poles,

Although these holdings
might never be relinquished,
I refuse to stay lakeside.

by Mary Langer Thompson

4:30 AM

Is it a barking dog
Or a screaming child crying for it's mother?
Is it cloudy outside
Or am I in a smoke filled room?
Is it that my heart is still beating
Or am I dead?
Is it California
Or Iraq
What day of the week is this
Someone tell me?
What a chain of thoughts
I have in my brain
I crave slumber
And freedom from contemplation
A clean slate
And a vacant box
Let me start all over again

by Tom Tipton

A Collection of Sound

A truck roars over a bridge
A pack of seagulls squark and caw across the bay
Coastal wind bashes against the window panes
Every door in the hour rattles
The refrigerator hums
Pachelbell's Canon floats smoothly from the house next door
Burnt leaves from an old chestnut tree whirl in the evening air
Kettle of chamomile tea brews and spouts on the stovetop;
it smells sweet, applelike, and aromatic; The kitchen is calm
Telephone in the bedroom rings and rings, but is never answered
An ambulance screams past the house
My cat murmurs peacefully on a green leather chair
Laughter of voices from the street draws me out to see
some kids return home on their bikes
Breaths out from riding; full of life
I want so much to find my own sound
Before the black night rolls in.

by Tom Tipton 7/23/19

The Pea Coat

Arranging the lost closet of clothes
you will no longer wear.
I come to find that old pea coat of yours.
The one you wore all the time like a suit of armor.
I took the coat to my nose.
This gesture endeared me to you absolutely.
In this visual world,
this modern landscape of polyester,
cotton, nylon, and pigment,
it is the smell inside this damn coat
that almost holds what's left of you.

by Tom Tipton

The Miracle of the Geese

Common birds, not thought of
as pretty, but look: the velvet soft blackness
of their necks, the bright white
of their cheek patches, coverts and mantle
layered down smooth like G-d
pressed flat the rough whorls of an oyster's shell,
breasts sporting the nacre sheen secreted
within that razored case—

These—stretched, a warning, a quivering arc—
even earthbound, are the wings of angels, surely:
built to carry ungainly things
to transfiguration on the air,
great grey flipper-feet forgotten
until the burn-dark primaries
lie folded away, gentled once more.

If you are still, if it is quiet
if you wait
if you sit, and do not move—
until your knees ache with it—
'til you bite your cheek
at the cold coming up
through the damp ground—
if you exercise
patience

(and maybe, if you pray),

if you are lucky, if they decide
you are not worth
their lacquer-eyed interest

you will hear the
dull-scissor sound
of their bills,
two fingers wide,
one finger long,
clipping the grass:

they graze,
close enough to touch
if you were a fool,
one watching
while the other
has its head down.

by Lauren Tyler-Rickon

The Ploughshare

Let me disabuse you
of the notion that a poem
is an elevated thing, rarefied,
not for everyday consumption.

This does not mean
it should not be well-wrought—
indeed, this is necessary,
is, by definition,
one of things a poem must be:
well-wrought.
It is right there, plain to see:
they are made things, poems,
made with some intended purpose,
like any other tool
made to fit the human hand
and ease our way
as we go naked through the world
with its thorns and stones,
and all its great vastnesses
that we do not understand.

I have been told that a poet
is a revolutionary:
the poet calls forth songs
from others' buried hearts,
and this makes it
a most dangerous creature.
Lest you think I am trying

to hang noodles on your ears,
Poets have been hunted,
have been assassinated,
in wilder times and places
than this one where we are.

I have been told a poem
can also be a sword.
And I, oh, I am angry.

I am angry, with all
the furious rage of a house
on fire, and with all the same
sodden, impotent loss
that comes after. I am angry.
And I am afraid.

There are so, so many things
for which this poem could become a sword:
should I choose, then,
the dried corpses of hummingbirds,
totems carried against the end
by aspirants going hard
across a desert they too may yet die in?
Or should I choose another?
It would take all the trees of Easter Island
all over again, and still it would not be enough
to list our endless, prideful, stupid sins.

I am sorry: I cannot give you an empty song
to blithely pass an idle hour.
But the world is a house afire already—

to give you another match,
what good would that do? Instead,
let me beat this poem into a ploughshare.
Our world has had enough,
and enough again, of swords.

See differently.
Love everything.
Do better.
That is all that we can do, and
that is what a poem is for:
a hand up from despair—
a crutch for the boredom-blinded eye.
Just a quiet, little song
to help the buried heart remember
what it already knows:
how to sing.

by Lauren Tyler-Rickon

TEOTIHUACAN
(Ancient Aliens)

Do not let them convince you
that we were nothing more than savages.
That only by the help of extraterrestrials
could we accomplish such magnificent feats.
The only empire whose construction relied on the help of "aliens"
is this one.

by Alexander Uribe

How To Become a Better Noodle Poet

Choose your noodle carefully.
Let's focus today on ramen -
other days we might groove
to curry laksa or saimin,
to guksu, bean threads, or pho.

For our noodle of choice,
immerse it in a delectable brew -
fish-based, pork-soaked, clear veggie
broths. Garnish with handfuls
of finely chopped scallions.

Build layers of tastiness,
from surface to secret interiors
add your own particulars -
pink fish cake, garden greens,
a perfectly poached egg yolk.

A memorable bowl of steaming
noodles can tantalize
all five senses, including
the ears as we listen
to our boisterous slurping.

Know that no two noodle-istas
compose the same song – no *your noodle
is better than mine* in this poet's kitchen -
learn to make every bite float
on the tongue, then dive.

by Amy Uyematsu

Echo in Monument Valley

to know you are loved
no matter
the object of affection
whether stone
desert stream
or a woman like me

to know you are loved
ancient secret
for shimmer
granite glint
water's swirl
this sheen on my cheek

by Amy Uyematsu

heartworks

~

lingering still
like that first kiss
before my trip north

~

two really bad falls
but now this soaring
a red-tailed hawk

~

usually so cautious
but to finally give in
dangerous yes

~

oceans apart
same blue sea
storm   calm   all of it

~

labor of love
is the hard hard work
of hearts connecting

~

the mystery is
not knowing why
but somehow sure

~
to still be adored
a lucky old girl
that's me

by Amy Uyematsu

Examination

In the aftermath of hurricane Dorian

A smell of fresh cut grass, I though,
identifying the load carried by breeze,
then as wind picked up
blown away images appeared in my phone
of non-people, non-houses,
non-existing communities.
Humans swept, buried, no longer there,
devastation complete,
survival, rebuilding I cannot imagine.
In the face of tragedy, I cry, open my wallet,
sorrow opens one's heart like no other key,
we're one, the same, it could happen to all.

Time passes,
labels resuscitate, identities expand
our breast with the pride of belonging.
I'm a European-Mediterranean woman,
not an Australian Aboriginal man,
language, gastronomical preferences,
my culture has been shaped, rooted by
stories of Carthaginians, Phoenicians, Greeks,
Romans, and all the ruined buildings left behind,
hemispheric theaters, roofless temples, decapitated gods,
alphabets, literature, the immeasurable deep blue
with sunken secrets still hidden from view.

How can a global-self integrate its manacled locality?
Ancestry encourage us to find who we are,
celebrate unexpected contributions to our DNA,
but let's not kid ourselves, labels separate.
Created to differentiate one category from another
hierarchy determines position by size, numbers,
attributes, some more appreciated than others.
When we belong to one group but not to another,
resent their appropriation of our music, literature,
history, language, how can we embrace them?

Before reaching school age
Hindu children are taught that they belong
to the cosmos, preventing identification with one religion,
one caste, one social status which would turn off
points of light, obscuring their malleable minds.
Can I, like the snake, shed this persona
fused to my being for over 60 years
to uncover the Self connected to all creation?
Will I be able to sing Rumi's lines,
I'm neither Christian nor Jew nor Magian nor Muslim...
sincerely saying:
I have put duality away and seen the two worlds
as One.
This is the only question.

by Alicia Viguer-Espert

Aurora

As a whisper of twilight reaches my window,
its open lips a promise of sweet peaches,
I listen to the diffused illumination
conversing with the ether.
Under Roman influence, Dawn,
already consecrated as a figure of speech,
didn't have a choice but to be renamed Aurora,
and stuck.

I remember my first encounter with Homer's image
a blind man with a cane wandering
from Asia Minor all the way to Athens,
how it lodged in my mind in cozy company
with the Three Wise Men and Baby Jesus.
Reading the Iliad, my father pointing a path on the atlas
coaxed me to picture the bard reciting long hexameters
to worthy men of state and the Greek citizenry.

Thanks to dad's obsession, Eos, The Rosy-Fingered One
remained plastered inside the walls of my child's brain.
Coming from a family of three siblings I imagined her
own family dynamics, how she got along with Helios
chatting as she opened the Gates of Heaven
every morning but with Selene, it was complicated.

As a kid I noticed clouds chameleonic transformation
to mauve-rose spaces under the novel effect of light
at the other extreme of the Mediterranean
in the Playa de La Malvarrosa,

the one frequently painted by Sorolla.
We children played with sand, light, breeze,
the lightness of being surrounded by centuries old
catastrophes still occurring today in our Sea.

Perhaps Homer never existed
but Dawn does,
and though Rome may have illegally appropriated
Eos' life turning her deeds and possessions to Aurora,
including her chariot, I salute the new goddess.
And when I get up early, always search the heavens
for signs of The Rosy-Fingered One about to perform
in the sky's stage her eternal, ever-new show.

by Alicia Viguer-Espert

New Day Dawning

Orange hue creeps up
on darkness and streams
through trees as the sky
slowly becomes brighter
giving hope to a new day

With a new dawn budding
a small breeze whispers
to the birds and nudges
them awake to sing

Brown squirrels scamper
amongst rocks hunting
for food before others arise

Waves crash on shore
in soft melodic tones
and spray seagulls
feeding in waters
and on sand

Sandpipers scurry
from pounding surf
searching for small prey
brought up from sea depths

The scene unfolds
like a painting come alive

while all breakfast
on the beach

by Lori Wall-Holloway

Originally published in a prior version *San Gabriel Valley Poetry Quarterly*, Fall, 2007

Light in the Storm

*"The light shines through the darkness,
and the darkness can never extinguish it." (John 1:5 NLT)*

A small vessel struggles
against the water's curl
as it strives to keep
the shore clearly in sight

Ocean waves rise and crash
beating against the boat's
starboard while winds
blow with a fierce hostility
causing a blinding spray
from the foamy sea

Thunder crashes
with clear power
Lightening bursts
through black
pregnant clouds
A lighthouse shines
its light to cut
through the darkness

The beam offers
guidance and shows
a clear route for lost
ships that fight
to stay afloat

by Lori Wall-Holloway

Shatter

I rearrange heirlooms inside
a hutch so their beauty
can be seen through the glass -
Clear crystal, bone china teacups
antique plates passed down
through generations

Over and over I arrange the items
like how I attempt to organize my life
So it looks just right; so it's flawless

But thoughts of where I failed
clutters my head
Rejection appears from deep
recesses of my brain

A tape plays inside my mind
"I can't be perfect if I'm a failure."

Instead of moving forward
I procrastinate
Why risk more negativity?
Why reach out to others?
Fear pushes me to quit trying
I decide to give up until –

SHATTER!!

Realization dawns and I am challenged

with false beliefs of myself versus what is real
who I really am

I don't need to be a model
of perfection to be validated
The One who created me will still
love and value me even when I make mistakes

I take a deep breath and recite
"Let my good be good enough,"
as I straighten a picture
on a crooked wall

by Lori Wall-Holloway

Originally published in a prior version *San Gabriel Valley Poetry Quarterly* Winter 2011 Issue 49

Welcome to the Occupation

by Chris Wallace

WHILE MOM&DAD
WERE ON THIER
PAID
STAY-CATiON
WELCOME
BACK INTO OUR
HOMELESS NATION
ONE HUNDRED
MILLION
STRONG and
STILL
GROWING

ALL YOU MILLENIALS
STILL LISTENING
CAN YHEAR A
BELL THAT'S
RINGING
?
THIS IS THE
GUILT
TRIP
GENERATION

WELCOME
TO
SUNNY
CALIFORNIA
IF YOU FILLED
OUT
an
APPLICATION

YOU CAN STAY
DRY
IF YOU WANNA
IF YOU HAVE TO
BUDDY
BUT HERE COMES
THE
RA!NY
SEASON

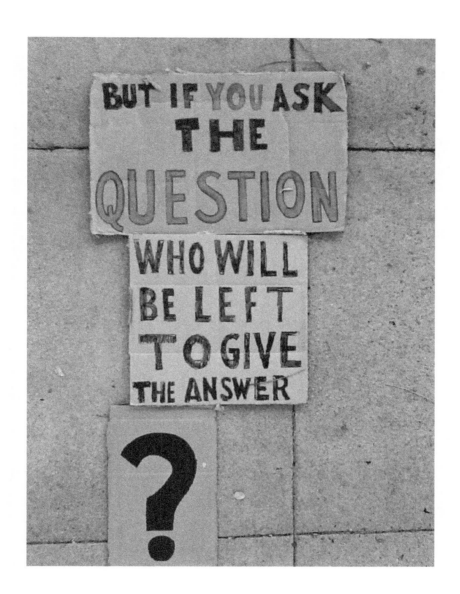

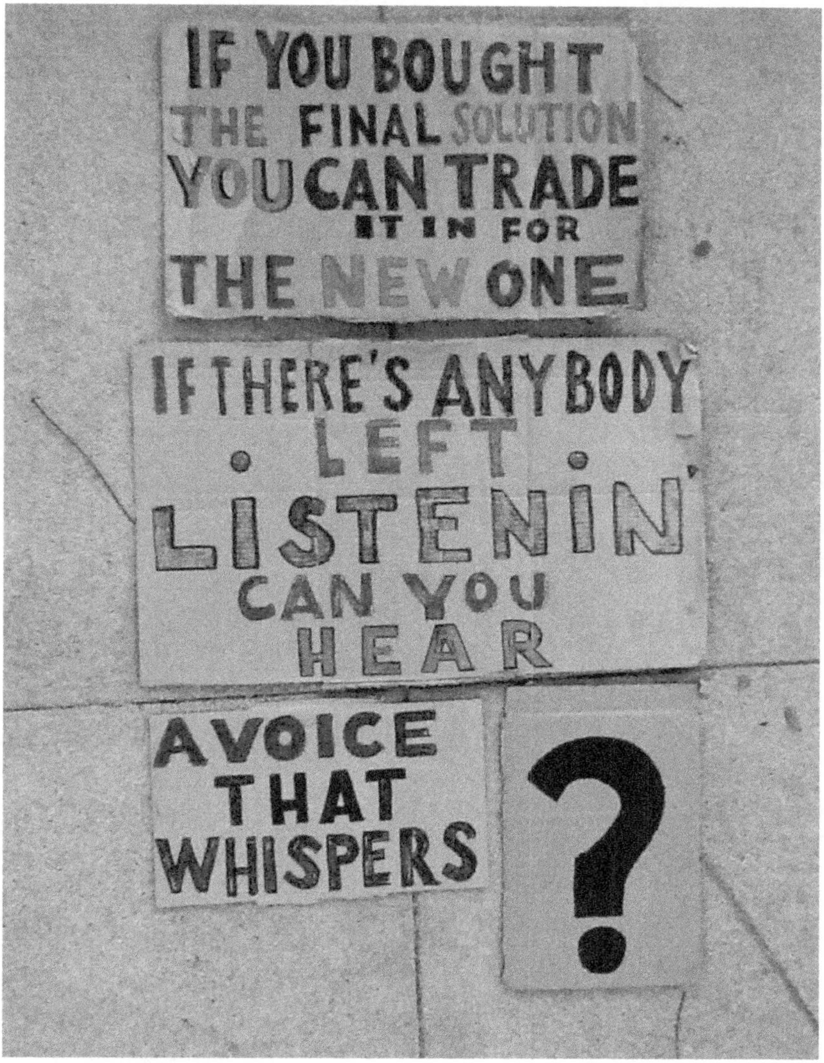
IF YOU BOUGHT
THE FINAL SOLUTION
YOU CAN TRADE
IT IN FOR
THE NEW ONE
IF THERE'S ANYBODY
LEFT
LISTENIN
CAN YOU
HEAR
A VOICE
THAT
WHISPERS
?

I Stole Your Roses

I stole your roses
Growing along the walk
Shamelessly sharing their scents
With the workmen, the dog walkers
and me
I stole them
The bright red bud, newly born
Hint of loveliness hidden
still wrapped
The perfectly petaled pink
pure and seductive
as a maiden
The yellow reflecting the sun
aloof, scentless
wearing morning diamonds
Mysterious and grand
the purple
deeper than lavender
lighter than royal
The white profusion of wedding veil
draping the fence with scent
and thorns
Altering my morning walk to pass
I stole them every day
You didn't notice
Clipping your eyes with pins
on the clothesline
Unaware of the loveliness
A little lower than your eyes

I stole them
Then watched the petals
Spread confetti on the walk
Smelling of city
But mine, saved
The lushness of full bloom
I stole your roses
And locked them in my soul

by Karen Whitmore

punctuation

he practiced punctuation
until his head was filled
sentences and paragraphs
his mother helped and drilled

periods commas colons
remembering each rule
getting ready for a test
in serious middle school

he slept with exclamation points
to emphasize his dreams
and caps to name the states
rivers and the streams

beginnings of sentences
and names of folks of fame
mrs so and so
and mama called by name

apostrophes for ownership
and putting words together
speaking less formally
by taking out a letter

what about a question mark
the squiggly shape that asks
for information wheres my book
or whats the coming task

quotation marks march in pairs
its dialogue says john
concluding with a period
before going on

his head filled with funny shapes
each designated place
a paragraph or sentence
or caps to note the case

what to wear to school my son
to help you be alert
keeping all these symbols straight
i want a lower-case shirt

by Karen Whitmore

Holy Jim

New Year's Day.
You
in winter uniform
tank top, cutoffs
as always
me, fearing cold
overdressed
in layers soon peeled away.
You shoulder them
as always.

Chaparral grasses bow and rise
in light, sage-scented Santa Anas
that lift your hair;
you in the lead
then I.

Each rise, new ridge
soothes with balm of
silencing distance
from city
unseen, deceivingly
close;
offers
vistas of an earth
in simpler times –
grasses
flowers
trees
man, woman
wind.

Segments
of the trail, darkly
cool in heat of noon -
tunnels
under branches, braided
more exquisite than a woman's hair
or any jeweled chain
about her neck.
Hidden from view -
barest touch of skin
a promise.

Our midday meal
cradled in a switchback
behind live oaks
feast
of almonds, crackers
grapes
heat-softened cheese
water.

Other trails past numbering
fold in upon each other
intersect, unite
beneath the inner sky -
veins pulsing
to the heart
as remembered taste of that repast
in a hairpin of a dusty path
births other scenes with you
past numbering
as in a dream.

Dawn.
I labor upward

on the Holy Jim
alone
sparingly layered
in company, it seems, of certain
cosmic constants - every trail
upward
every walk
alone
but carrying, of late
a talisman -
small pebble, white
rounded, reassuring
pulled from trailhead dust
and glinting in the early light
like hope
a pearl
pocketed
to speed the advent
of a time when scent of sage
will conjure images of only
sage.

Maybe soon.

Perhaps today.

by Terry Wilhelm

What All The World Is

Out on the patio
our table faces a twelve-foot doorway
in the high wall.
Sun brightens the sidewalk.
A clean, green vista; shadows of leaves
moved by breezes grace the grass.
Occasional cars pass.
Man on cell phone paces by.
One direction, then the other.
Volume cranked to max for each pronouncement.
For his private listener? For us?
He doesn't look our way, but
his peacock preening
in the spotlight of life
reaches us
more clearly than his voice.
Soon joined
by a fellow pacer
a woman, intent on her conversation;
slightly quieter than he, but still
loud enough.
We can't see the intersection of their passing.
Which is the star
and which the supporting actor?
Is one upstaging the other?
Do their loud-levels wax as they near
each other?
Finally
she disappears

and
not soon enough
he, too.
We can't help but laugh
at the unintended comedy.

by Terry Wilhelm

Her Place

Sometimes carried like a baby, sometimes rolling off a van like a favorite
float in the rose parade, she made it every week to the Japanese Garden to
read her poems. It was her place, she said. She was quiet with a twinkle
and a wild side. She wrote about how she was the one who slid off the roof
onto the back of the family pig and rode it bareback. She was invincible, and
no one knew her age. I've traveled to 116 countries so far, she said. When I
told the gardener. . .his *oh no*! turned into woodwork. He widened a space
on the small poetry meeting vista by the ponds. A poetry chair, he said,
in the meditation place. Carved lovingly into the back, her name already,
if only she could see.

no longer
a wheel chair
now that she could fly

by Kath Abela Wilson

Akitsu Quarterly, Summer, 2019

Redwood Driftwood

she kept it
phut

At water's edge
on this hidden beach
ancient creatures gather.
Immense, in their isolation
their untouched bodies
have grown old.
They lie together,
making shadows
amidst the splintered remains of giants.
I walk on their backs, from one to the other.
Their long silence before the ocean's roar
has carved three sandy coves in the high stone cliffs.
I enter each,
and leave no footsteps.
One, dark, with eagle's head
and younger than the rest,
rises up, surveying,
as if to find its cry.

by Kath Abela Wilson

Loving Caretakers

"We took a long drive into the hills. I never had said I love you. She seemed distant and I was unsure. There were small stalls along a rustic road, vegetables and fruit. We struck a chord. I pulled over. They gave us little paper cups and poured them full of real apple cider, a heady brew. Our first drink, first kiss, that settled it." More than fifty years later he told me that story as he eyed his wife wishing they could travel. They lived their first year in an open-air teahouse on his parents' grounds, inherited a paradise, and out of the goodness of their hearts, made it a public garden. Open days and weddings, their own long postponed honeymoon. Instead they build a room for the bride to dress.

garden tour
even the buddha
has some regrets

by Kath Abela Wilson

Hedgerow #106, 2017

I pray

I resent the potus
To keep peace of mind
I pray for him
Not for his sake
But for mine

by Joe Witt

Kite Boarder

gliding on water
skimming the top of the waves
the kite boarder rides
leaving troubles behind
in its shimmering wake

by Joe Witt

Benediction

She prayed for them
They
Prayed for rain
for climate change
like warmer winters
cooler summers

They
prayed for better sons and brighter daughters
for perfectly cooked meals
and to shed a few pounds
so they would drop several dress sizes

She prayed for them
They
prayed for closure; to move on
after the loss of spouses
for less incontinence
for more comfort after cancer

They
prayed for grandchildren and grace
that arrives gently; like dew at dusk
for family to surround them
when their soul surrendered

She prayed for them

They
kneeled in closets, at bedsides
on fabric facing east
spoke intercessorily
in unmitigated elocution

They
assembled in synogogues, temples, and sanctuaries
waded in the water, gathered at river banks
sent flowers to sea, synchopated hand splashes
summoned the Holy Spirit to me

She prayed them
safe
She prayed them
free
She prayed them
to the Father

She prayed them
gone
The last mile of the way; at twilight
She prayed them
home!

by C. Jerome Woods

Two Black Men

(Has Society Gone Mad?)

Today there was no fanfare, balloons, nor grandstand
But spontaneity and brotherhood prevailed
No news media, Not KTLA, not TeleMundo, not KCET
Yet, History was being made.

Down the street from West Angeles Cathedral
Where Bishops reign
And choirs "sang"
Down the street from Chef Marilyn's, the Living Room, Pep Boys,
Walgreen's, Starbucks,
Denny's, that corner-stoned the AHF billboard that
Greg and I proclaimed.

Down from Lula Washington's Dance Studio, Sebastian Ridley-Thomas'
office and Angelus Funeral Home
We made History!

Up the street from the Vision Theatre, Ackee Bamboo,
Barbara Morrison's Music Academy,
Art + Practice, Ben Caldwell's KAOS,
Regency West, and Zambezi

Up from ghosts remembering Venusian Salon, Cindy Lu's, Leimert Park
Beauty College and Mrs. Wells,
5th Street Dicks, Lucy Florence's twins Ron & Richard, Brockman
Gallery's Alonso & Dale,

Jimi Walton's Gallery, Ramsess, parade Grand Marshal - dancer and
actor, West Gale.

Spirit recalling the do's, don'ts, and wee hours of the morning dealings

We did it!

Near Maverick's Flat that sits across from what used to be the
Centerfield
At the intersection of past covenants, new cultures and consciousness,
traffic, construction, and gentrification
Same Gender Loving (SGL) versus gay
Oftentimes, it be's that way.

We did it!

Where National Shirt Shop, Ontra Cafeteria, the Broadway, May
Company once stood
Where the bust of bondsman, activist, community champion/Celeste
King keeps watch
Where capricious consumers cross ground zero
Where the Metro #40 turns; east of the Blvd. Crenshaw headed to
Downtown L. A.
Where the #705 Rapid turns south; onto the "Shaw" from MLK Blvd.
that once answered to Santa Barbara Ave.

We did it!

No high tea
Just Paul, and me
Two Black Men

No pinky raised, no slurps, no sips.
Today, as Jehovah Witnesses read, Muslim brothers fed
The Po-Po on motorcycles sped
Where urban dwellers exhibited tattoos, amidst bandanas of
blue and red.

1:30 PM lunch hour; he kissed me on the lips.

No "Big Brother" helicopter, no twelve gun salute, no "drive-by" either

We did it!

Two Black Men made History!

Two Black Men shared love!

… of family

of friends

of community

of humanity

of my man

and me …

This IS a LOVE poem!

by C. Jerome Woods

Eclipsed

Ivory moon slowly fades into earth's shadow
Turns a reddish hue, color of blood.
In the darkness, the cry of wolves.
Wind drives through the chaparral,
Fierce and defiant.

Traveling home, I smell the scent of skunks
Struck dead on the highway.
Moon didn't protect them.
Nocturnal animals, wild, unfit for shelters,
Musk not strong enough to repel danger.

White stripes blaze down black backs.
In the shadows, death lurks--
         Sudden
      Random.

by Nina Yamamoto

Farewell

Mother, you were a pearl of abundance
That night you smiled weakly
Snow falls on hidden landscapes
Your scrawled writing, not a red flag.

That night you smiled weakly
The future, an unknown haze
Your scrawled writing, not a red flag.
Not aware you had suffered trauma.

The future, an unknown haze
Don't believe I could have changed your fate
Not aware you had suffered trauma.
Desert rose cloistered in shrouds.

Don't believe I could have changed your fate
Your eyes were closed, you couldn't speak
Desert rose cloistered in shrouds
Dreams of the past, confusion.

Your eyes were closed, you couldn't speak
Brain scan showed cerebral hemorrhage
Dreams of the past, confusion
You showed a delicate strength.

Brain scan showed cerebral hemorrhage
Life's sorrows, muted shadows
You showed a delicate strength
You cared for family and friends.

Life's sorrows, muted shadows
Mother, you were a pearl of abundance
You cared for family and friends
Snow falls on hidden landscapes.

by Nina Yamamoto

Homesickness

René Magritte, 1940

Golden haze,
Other worldly light,
Neither day nor night,
On a bridge
He stands, dreams
Maple leaves, burning
At a lion's feet.

Fallen angel
Doesn't belong here.
Silent, black attire
Heavy, bird-like wings.
He gazes out
Hears only the ebb and flow
Of black water
Unceasing.

Lion's face reflects light
A new freedom,
Kingly majesty.
He could look human,
Sport a black tie,
But remember only his last meal
Antelope and hummingbird nectar.

by Nina Yamamoto

Garden of Snow Peas

I taught kindergarten students to plant snow peas in a parent's backyard. We came every other day to water and watch the peas grow into vines. The class was delighted when the pink and purple snow peas blossomed. Everyone wanted to pick the flowers for their mothers. I told them to wait for the snow pea pods to grow behind each blossom. That completed the life cycle of the delicious snow peas that we ate, both raw and stir fried.

in springtime, my children
plant tiny snow pea seeds
pink and purple blossoms
fill the garden
crunchy pea pods complete the cycle

by Sharon Yee

Haibun with haiku
Milton Quon Watercolor Artist

Milton Quon as a child always was drawing, sketching and doodling. A family friend advised his parents to allow him to follow his passion so he would always be happy. He went to art school on a scholarship. He was a very hard worker with a sense of humor and a gentle demeanor. He worked for Disney Studio on "Fantasia" and "Dumbo". He taught art, was a commercial advertising artist,and a fine artist in watercolor painting. When asked his secret for one hundred and five years of life, he replied," Marry a good Chinese wife, eat Chinese food, and go to churchie." He was a loved family man with three sons and one daughter, and four grandsons. Milton loved to show the play of lights in his paintings God said, "let there be light and there was light and there was Milton."

one hundred and two year old
cartoon animator
learning to fly with Dumbo

by Sharon Yee
Published by *Haiku Society of America*, 2016 Members' Anthology *Full of Moonlight*

Prose

My Own Special "Summer of Love"

"Experience," according to one definition, "is what we get when we don't get what we wanted."

While 1967 is considered the "Summer of Love," it was the following summer when Marian enchanted me. She was—in my eyes—the exemplar of femininity: ash blonde hair falling around a smooth face with full lips and a turned-up nose, almond eyes, and a womanly body (or at least as close as one at 16 can get). She captured my teenaged heart at a local party. She lived five blocks away, but I'd never met her before because I attended boarding school.

That summer was when Marian enchanted me. I <u>had</u> to go out with her.

Adolescent obsession firmly ensconced, I dedicated summer to "wooing and winning" her, attending any neighborhood party where she might appear, hanging around or near anywhere she spent time, even inviting her out on my sailboat "Chloe" (named somewhat aptly for the Greek goddess of summer fertility). My favorite song became the Beatles' "Hey, Jude," taking its lyrics as a sign we were meant to be together since they advise one to not focus on negative outcomes while acting on feelings and fearlessly allowing vulnerability—without all that psychobabble.

That summer provided some manic moments. I balanced behavior between beastly lust and gentlemanly propriety, playing it "cool," to whatever extent a 16-year-old is capable of in trying to restrain youthful fawning. She responded to questions about her interests, hobbies, and hopes softly but indifferently, politely brushing me off. I ignored reality: every smile meant she cared, that I was making my way into her life. I envisioned Marian taking the two-hour train ride to visit me as my girlfriend during weekends off or my date at social functions.

Still, I was running out of time. School restarted in another month; I had to harvest whatever good will was present to have any chance.

So I conjured up enough courage to ask her out.

"You know," I said, feigning nonchalance. "We should go somewhere this weekend."

"Huh?"

"Want to go out?"

"No," she intoned.

"Huh?" Now *I* was doing it.

"No," she repeated apathetically.

Testily, I asked why.

"Because I have no interest in being with you."

Ducking under the arm I'd propped against a tree she was leaning on, she sauntered toward the dock where our friends were. Although numbed silent, it wasn't long before insult ("How could she reject me?") simmered into animosity ("Who does she think she is?"), finally exploding into anger ("How dare she?").

I unleashed fury at the situation into my fists and out. The target? I began hitting the tree, striking its trunk repeatedly, alternating punches in a frenzy, channeling bile into each blow. Eventually, my hormone-driven passion wore off as I registered the pain from the 15 or 20 blows taken against an entirely innocent tree.

Once I stopped, I saw the results.

The knuckles on both hands looked like raw hamburger, meaning more than my heart broke that afternoon. So did several layers of skin. The tree, on the other hand, stood as before. Aside from some chipped bark, it remained unchanged and certainly unaffected. Clearly, my reactions against the injustice of reality hadn't affected my victim but had certainly damaged me.

While it was not a good moment, it proved a productive experience. In hindsight, my rage resulted from disappointment, realizing I'd squandered the past two months in self-delusion.

Now, I can recall that "relationship" with a sort of fondness because it taught me the best way to recover from a broken heart: simply move on, seek another's company. In fact, about a dozen years later, after relocating from New York to Florida, one of my first dates declared, "I don't know if we should go out. After all, you're a Yankee."

I doubt she expected the shrug I gave as I replied, "That's up to you. Guess it depends on how important it is to you."

The pain from a break-up of a relationship that never really existed taught me what every teenager should know and more importantly understand: what we feel in the moment is just that—momentary; whatever personal pain we endure does not last forever.

And for that, I thank Marian.

by Bill Cushing

Dawn Robin

I was born at dawn and the robins were singing. My mother said she used to bathe me in the tide pools. I lost her to breast and lung cancer. After she had her breast removed, she asked her best friend to smuggle a pack of cigarettes into the hospital. Being young and not addicted to anything stronger than television and chocolate, I couldn't understand her actions.

As I write here, I am 57 and addicted to the bastards myself! My father, she claimed, was an armed robber with a touch of pyromania and a fondness for the greyhounds and gambling. A bum she said who never worked a day in his life. She claimed he would charge her to babysit me. He wanted a boy she said. There was a big 8x10 in a crummy silver frame..me...dressed up like a boy in a sailor suit...complete with hat. Boys' clothes.

Growing up in San Diego was cool I guess. I loved listening to the radio... Making up school- crush songs and dancing in front of my mirror. I was convinced I was going to be a star. Dad left when I was three. No brothers or sisters...it was just me & mom. I wanted to find out about this Jesus people were singing about. My mother having had her fill of the hypocrisy of organized religion...said when you are 18, you can pick one. A year or so later, I begged her to take me inside a nice looking church we passed on our way home. She wouldn't hear of it. I still wasn't sure who Jesus was when she died. But I was mad as hell at this God who would take away my only parent...my only source of love.

I became a ward of the court in the city of San Francisco. When temporary group homes weren't available, the city had no choice but to put me in the runaway section of juvenile hall alongside the real runaways and juvenile delinquents upstairs. Suddenly an orphan in a world of sin. They had a semi-broken down piano there. I started to fiddle around on it. I don't know one note from the next but I managed to come up with a two handed piano piece. Sad...dramatic...& slow with a jazzy syncopated bit thrown in at the end for kicks. I carried this melody to each and every piano I came across....faithfully...all throughout my life.

I went down a dark road of drug addiction. Riding a wave of self-destruction and rebellion, I contracted gangrene & septic shock poisoning. I was laying on the floor dying unable to get warm. Even though it was summer and 102 degrees outside I had a winter coat on and a space heater blasting in the afternoon. My boyfriend at the time said he heard the voice of God saying go to her she needs you. When I got to the hospital they couldn't get my blood pressure up and the gangrene was traveling to my heart. At first, they said they were going to chop off my arm to the elbow and give me a metal hook all the way down. But as my condition worsened, as I came closer to death, they had my boyfriend at the time say his last goodbyes. According to him...a doctor who had a glow about him came in and tried one last thing. It saved my life and my arm! Why? Because I believe that God In His Infinite Wisdom gave me that song and just a few months later melody to carry throughout my life. If I had died or even had to hook up to my elbow on my left arm, it would have been much more difficult to find myself at the baby grand piano in the sanctuary of Gardena International Church Composing through the power of the Holy Spirit the song savior. I believe God knew it all along. A beautiful young bride came to me and asked for permission to perform the song for the children at an orphanage in Haiti as she danced with metal balls that she would light on fire and she thought it would speak to them.

I continue to write songs and consider myself God's Songbird my name is Dawn Robin I was born at dawn and the robin's were singing.

by Dawn Robin English

Invasion of the Painted Ladies

It's so rare to find life on a Los Angeles freeway, and sure you can say that every driver is alive, but let's be honest, behind the wheel we are mindless as robots, zombified. Unless, of course, someone drives too slow because they just have to text their brains out or another zombie cuts them off. Then there is life—the middle-fingered Hobbesian kind.

But on a gloomy March in the middle of rush hour, swarms of painted ladies flutter between the gridlock like French youth biking lazily to the farmer's market, their loose hair and bare thighs glistening in the breeze.

It was a particularly rainy season in Southern California, and a little depressing — Trump's 3rd fucking year, teachers in the streets, #metoo malaise — and then the painted ladies appeared in droves, a blasphemous beauty, dancing between the closed windows of our cars where we ritualize our rugged American deaths. O harbingers of hope lead me to that other life!

by Emily Fernandez

Berkeley Drive

A cypress grows behind a front yard fence. Behind that tree, a house, a single floor, a stucco cube. The shades are drawn, the walls are gray and magazines peek out from the mailbox. The sun warms Berkeley Drive. It's 4 p.m. Nothing is at risk.

Of a childhood friend, Cszeslaw Milosz wrote: *He sought strong flavors. He fled from kitsch.* Still, Milosz's wartime friend can't have been the last. Berkeley Drive is far from 1940, very far from Poland. But why not another, here on this block?

Scan the street. Look out for someone drawn to resinous scents. Look for a serious face – serious, but skeptical.

Yours, for instance. Don't you seek strong flavors? Don't you shrink from sentiment? Aren't you convinced of the past and its power? Don't you sometimes wonder whether neighbors are drawn toward history's klieg-lit heat, like moths towards nightmare?

Our parents fled the East. They came of age in winter: they imagined months of sunshine, hot enough to burn light into the shadows.

Let me confess: I don't know whether that tree is really a true cypress, genus *Cupressus*. The tree doesn't care: like many living things, it answers to more than its given name. We don't need its name to love its fragrance.

There, at least, is a saving grace.

by Tom Laichas

Murmur

She was on the ragged edge of sleep, in those dark
velvety moments just before dawn, in the small, crowded
bedroom of the old Spanish bungalow on Vista Grande.
The small bedroom she shared with her sister, and a year
later with a newborn baby brother. Her dark-eyed sister,
Nicole, lay sleeping in the twin bed, which ran crosswise
at the foot of her own long, narrow bed. Curled up on
her side, facing the wall, with its swirls of white wedding
cake plaster, straight black hair in pink rubber curlers,
her older sister slept, unaware, undisturbed.

Some unidentifiable murmur in the dark and distant
garden with its tangle of fruit trees and brick edged,
moss covered, herring bone pathways, had awakened
her, terrified her. She lay there shaking under her thin
blanket, sobbing into the softness of a feather pillow,
encased in its delicately embroidered slip. Sewn by
a grandmother who lived far away, but dreamt of her
nightly, and sent beaded moccasins at Christmas and
braid ties and bows for her birthday.

A light went on in the turquoise and gray tiled, deco
bathroom that separated the master bedroom from the
small room with its textured, white walls and large picture
window. The room they called the nursery. The warm
glow from the nightlight spilled out into the room, from
the crack beneath the door, with its crystal doorknobs.
Shadows danced menacingly across the iced walls.
There was that sound again. Then the door opened,
and her mother's arms were around her. Petting her,
smoothing her hair, brushing her tawny bangs from her

313

forehead. Patting her on the back.
Whispering 'shhh' into her tiny ear,
"There baby, don't cry."
She almost sang the words, tender and somewhat
out of key. Then the sound again.
"Coo-coo coo-coo, "
"It's just a mourning dove calling to his mate."
"Coo-coo coo-coo"
She had not the slightest idea what a mourning dove was,
but she believed her, she trusted her, she had no
reason not to, yet. The child stopped crying as she
breathed in her mother's perfumed aroma now full of
the musky scent of sleep and dreams. Then the small
body in the vastness of the twin bed, relaxed in her
mother's arms, as tears were wiped from her emerald,
thick-lashed eyes, first with gentle finger tips, then the
silky corner of a blue chenille dressing gown.

The young mother slipped into the narrow bed with the
child, kissed away the remaining tears, and held her
tightly against her breast, until she drifted off once more
into the unparalleled safety of sleep.
"Coo-coo Coo-coo"

~~~~~~~*~~~~~~~

Years later, lying naked, in a spacious, antique, wooden bed in a
bougainvillea-covered villa, in Tuscany, the woman who grew from
the child, would tell her lover, this was her earliest memory.

by Sharmagne Leland-St. John

First Published: *Unsung Songs* ~ A First Collection of Poetry (*Quill and Parchment Press* ~ 2001)

Invisible to Myself

The North Hollywood Red Line ran back and forth from the 7th Street Metro station all night, it seems, or at least it did last night.

3 AM found me head down, arms sprawled, on my seat. The older, bearded, black man across from me had hardly moved for the last hour.

I exchanged a gaze with a large transit officer through the window as I quickly sat up.

This was my third straight night of riding L.A.'s after prime time follies, the tragedy without names or ratings.

The self-esteem had taken a beating. I had a hard time looking at myself in the mirror.

The officer acknowledged the inevitable. The growing chasm between the number of homeless and the city's ability to do anything about them.

I had never in my 42 years felt the disappointment and shame I did then. My parents' dreams for a happy and contented life for me seemed to have gone haywire since escaping to Hollywood from the small, but overpopulated, independent living center in Carson, CA with $50

in my hand.

I had spent the last 20 years of my life acting, writing, telling jokes and singing. Now, my attempt at finally making money from what I loved had hit Tinseltown's underbelly like a dead pigeon.

The land of dreams had turned into the valley of demons, most of my own making.

I had left New York City a few weeks earlier to rid myself of the wannabes and you-don't-know-until-you-tries that had haunted me for so long.

This, my 24th trip to Los Angeles, would find me atop Laurel Canyon as just another near carcass.

I knew down deep, however, that the city I so loved and admired had iron jaws this time around.

On Tuesday, my fourth straight day of wandering, the whispers and frustrations of Angelinos came full force.

Exiting the Beverly/Vermont Metro station in dirty gray New York Rangers sweatshirt and torn white plastic bag holding all of my earthly possessions, a large Hispanic man selling wares launched into a long and passionate diatribe aimed at me.

I told him to "go fuck yourself."

This aimless roaming and rousting about with the universe, had changed me. It made me mean.
Made me bitter. Made me need to stand up for myself at every corner and declare that I am
alive, I do matter, and I will never not make a difference.

The two ladies near the bus stand on Vermont had the final word.
"At least," the older one said to the younger, "he doesn't have to take off that shirt here."

I felt like I was beginning to lose something much more precious than a sweatshirt.

If I hadn't lost it already.

by Radomir Vojtech Luza

Underwater

I am living underwater, again, or did I ever leave? Opening my eyes in the ocean that sparkles lemon in a sunrise, I can't see. I wait for midnight to unpeel my eyelids in a blackness and breathe. I'm sunk at the bottom of the sea, sifting in sand beds for seashells that have drifted into a darkness, detached and vacant.

I still remember colors, the way the sun glows like a tangerine on fire at sunset, arsonists bowing to the sleep of a star. I remember blood in my body like rubies mined from India, where wombs grew in wombs. I remember the moon like a pearl snatched from a necklace and tossed away from Earth, pulling tides in the ocean, washing seaweed up to shore.

If you want to know what it's like down here I will tell you. Fill your sink basin with tap water, submerge your eyes wide open, letting particles from the pipe shift across your membranes. It looks like a murky reservoir water with water babies splashing in bathing suits with mommies and sinking to sand beds where I keep them.

Water babies swim laps in the uterus and dive onto the planet. They are placed on a breast and left there, they suck milk that is sweet till it goes sour. Anything good goes bad—chunks of milk cheese splatting onto steel and mixing with dishwater, swirling down pipes, and shuttling particles to the ocean where I keep them. There's nothing but black inside a blackness, lemons covered in mold, hiding golden peels. Love what is that? How do you know when you're in it and then out? It doesn't last.

Mango trees and white womb walls housed my mother. She is a soul divided into billions, yet a temple. We mined rubies in India and called them ours, draping them around our necks and letting them clatter against our collarbones, setting fire to fire in the blood orange of a sunset. I remember the way our palms fit together and squeezed crossing the street. I am a seashell, losing things that weren't mine to begin with, left with souls smashed into pipe particles, draining to the ocean where I lie.

I am living underwater, again, I left once but returned like the moon clawing its way back to Earth, smashing waves against cliff walls in protest of an exile. You can't keep tides from coming. The sleep of a star is my morning. At midnight I unpeel my eyelids inside blackness and breathe.

by Roshan Zoe Moazed

Sun daughters

Sun daughters hang around my neck like an anchor made of cement harvested from the sidewalk where shoes of a species step, mindless of marigolds sparkling apricot and scarlet, growing beneath their feet in the golden hour before sunset.

I cannot ignore them, chewing into my eyeballs and mouth trying to make me own the light in my name that was claimed back in Persia before Iran and revolutions drove daddies from the desert and flew them smashed in planes to Ohio.

Sun daughters were new. They had never seen suns in a flower, or cradled marigolds in palms still crusty from desert heat and smelling of cardamom. Never held something that looked like sunset painted on petals. Weeping, they pressed flowers to their cheeks and stroked stems.

My name was written in calligraphy centuries ago, before Ohio where dads sat in lawn chairs sipping a drink called lemonade that rolled off their tongue, funny and sour. Drinks that pulled our fathers farther from their origins where sticky dates fell into fingers and cardamom was ground fresh, filling kitchens with the scent of a home and rosewater.

My name was illuminated by the sun on a Sunday by beams of sunset blending into pink. And suddenly I was apricot and scarlet like flowers pushing through soil, like the star that pulls the planet. Though I wished for blackness, I was bright, blinded by myself and the soul. Sun daughters bloomed from my breasts as I screamed.

Sun daughters had never seen the sun in a flower. So they wept, naming me after light shattering through windowpanes and lighting wallpaper on fire. Now I am sun daughter though I pray for the moon to relieve me, letting me sink into nighttime, black as the sky that was before my name was written in calligraphy centuries ago to place the sun star, pulling the planet in ellipses of year rounds.

Though I don't want it, I am light, apricot and scarlet sprouting from dirt, housing sunset in my hair, starlight in my pupils reminding the Earth of Persia, of daddies in Ohio with glasses of lemonade too sour, of golden hours before the sun releases me to night. I am named the light. And so I am.

by Roshan Zoe Moazed

A Room of My Own

After reading Virginia Woolf's, book, *A Room of One's Own*, I became enthralled with creating my own space. She wrote, "women must have money and privacy in order to write." Woolf's focus was on women with literary genius, not the ordinary woman who lacked money and competence. She also wrote, "money cannot be earned; it must come to the writer in the form of a windfall or a legacy or it will bring with it attachments, obligations."

Years ago I came into a six-figure windfall that allowed me to convert a third bedroom into a space of my own. It was a third bedroom being used as a storage room. I could now clean it out and make space for me to read, write, and create. At the time I didn't know how or what to write until I started attending writing workshops and began to recall childhood memories. A facilitator at one of those workshops told me that she thought I had writing talent and introduced me to her agent. That's when writing memoir began to take hold and having a room of my own became important.

I phoned the Salvation Army to make arrangements for them to haul away the stained gray camelback sofa, the old desk and chairs. The floor was covered with stacks of books that needed organizing. I headed to Ikea in Burbank in search of a new sofa and a bookcase. Finding a sofa was an unsuccessful journey, but happily I found the perfect bookcase, paid $250, and scheduled an appointment for delivery and installation. Within two days Ikea was at my door. The delivery men unpacked it, screwed it to the floor and wall for earthquake safety, and I could see change beginning to take place. The stacks of books that covered the floor now had a home.

The search for a sofa continued. I found a short white sofa with two huge pillows on display in the window of a small European furniture boutique in Pasadena, paid $600 for it, and arranged for next day delivery. Excitement was taking hold with this conversion project of creating a room of my own.

Next I found a desk with an adjustable chair on sale at Staples in Monrovia and paid $120 for the set. My husband and I loaded them onto his truck for free transport home. Now I needed to get rid of the dusty old window blinds. Realizing that Calico Corners fabric store was nearby in Arcadia, I headed over and found the perfect Bohemian fabric for curtains and coordinating pillow covers. I quickly paid the cost for my order, came home and decided to have my windows and carpet professionally cleaned for $200.

Within days of the window washing and carpet cleaning, Ed, from Calico Corners showed up with my new curtains draped over his right arm and rods in his left hand. I was thrilled. This was the last and most expensive touch at $800 for the room of my own.

It felt good not having to ask my husband for his approval or his money. It meant no second opinions, no arguments, no attachments, no obligations. As my room began to take hold I no longer saw myself as ordinary and incompetent. I began to dream of becoming the literary genius in Woolf's book.

by Toni Mosley

The Boy and His Bird

The boy and his bird sat on the bench. They watched the rain wash down the street, brown leaves and pink plastic bags flowing through the storm drains. The white rain ran through cracks in the asphalt, oscillating like tide pools. Dead bugs rose and fell in these pools, occasionally pushed down the street by the force of the wind.

The boy wore only jeans and a thin hoodie with a long tear across his chest. The edges of this tear were frayed, as if he needled with them, but at this moment, and during every previous moment, his hands lay flat against his legs. The raven rested on the boy's shoulder, black feathers slick like oil. The boy's skin was marred and rough, his hair curled and untamed underneath his hood.

A shriveled old woman sat hunched on the bench beside the boy and his bird. She had a dollar store shawl wrapped around her head, a plasticine silk patterned with pink snakes.

"Where are you headed?" The bird asked, and the woman cracked her bones.

"Wherever the bus takes me," she said, and the raven nodded in agreement.

The sky was a hazy white, and fat milky drops splattered onto the pavement at the boy's feet. His shoes, thin-soled Converse with the laces untied, were soaked all the way through, and his heel poked through a hole in the back. He was soaked to the bone, the white clearly defined, as if his skin stuck to his skeleton as the plastic bags to the street.

"Boy," the raven cawed, pecking at his ear. "When does the bus arrive?"

"Whenever the last bus leaves," he replied, eyes unmoving from the divot against the opposite curb where a bag full of pink leaves rose and fell with the wind.

The old woman stood suddenly, her hunched figure forgotten as the scarf around her head was torn away by the whispering wind. The silent voices grew louder as her fingers and toes began to grow longer, her nose sharper, her bones bending and stretching against her skin.

The boy and the bird watched as she became undone, no longer any trace of human left inside her. Rivulets of blood and chunks of bone washed away down the street, ribbons of skin turning and writhing like snakes.

The red of the blood and the white of the rain made a soft pink that looked like strawberry milk, the ichor of children.

The boy let out a deep sigh and the raven burrowed its face into the crease of his neck, its cold beak pressing against the exposed skin between his hoodie and hair. He brought his hand onto the bird's back and felt the feathers beneath his fingers.

"Do you think the bus will ever come?" The raven asked the boy. "A year, a decade, a century, an eon we've been waiting, and for what?"

"We wait for the bus to come and the storm to end," the boy said.

"But for how long?" the raven cried.

"Look around you Raven," he said. "There is nothing else here."

The bird opened his eyes for the first time and looked. All he saw was the bus rising up over the horizon and the break of sun in the sky.

by Elliott Lee Negrin

Bronte

When I hear the word Bronte, two British girls come to mind. Women writers. And of course windy hills, heather, northern romance.

Bronte is not an English name, though. Born South—under a volcano—it means 'rumble'. It refers to the moaning guts of our mother earth when she's discontent, about to erupt lava on her kids.

Bronte is a verdant feud the Spanish gave to the British (uncaring of the fact the folks who lived there weren't Spanish or British). The land was handed down like a precious stone, green with olives and grapes, starred with the gold of citrus trees.

It's a shame that—due to fake promises, misplaced words of revolution—riots flared beyond control and some well-off people were killed. Do I feel for them? Yes. The slaughtering of civilians is called a massacre.

I ask myself if their living a quite leisurely life, prior to their untimely death, is a mitigating factor. I guess not. Is it normal to be born into privilege and deem it right? It must be. I don't know of many exceptions to the rule.

What about those five peasants shot against a wall, the day after? None of them, to later inquiry, was proved guilty of anything. All bore the same first name, matched with an assortment of local patronymics. Was it by chance?

They were all named Nunzio—that signifies 'angel'. Is there meaning behind the coincidence? Does history still itself for a second, if we dare repeating these names out loud, calmly spelling these five letters five times? Or does it keep going?

What about the fifth Nunzio, whom none of the soldiers dared to shoot? He was the village fool and a boy. Even feuds the Spanish donated to the English have fools… neither Spanish nor English, of course.

No one fired at the fool, but he didn't realize it. Not quite. When he found himself still alive—was he, truly?—he just kneeled down and wept, arms thrust towards the sky. He cried tears of joy, muttering thanks to the Virgin who, knowing him innocent, had apparently graced him. Knowing him sinless, pure, incapable of evil, Mary-Mother-of-God had shielded him. She had kept him unscathed.

On his knees, he sung praises to Heaven under the scorching sun—in the dusty plaza that Goya could have painted, if he were around—when the General-of-Our-Resurgence arrived and took things in his hands. He hovered above the kid and cold-bloodedly shot him in the head.

Is it what makes a hero, I wonder? For I have honored the man as such since elementary school. His name printed in bold, etched in stone, a pride of the nation. Is it what true heroism means?

What about the lawyer who wasn't called Angel but—being Bronte's most literate native—was accused of riotous intentions then jailed, waiting for execution? When news came of his complete uninvolvement he was released on parole. Friends begged him to leave. He remained for justice to take its course. He was shot for good measure.

I never saw his name on a street plaque, not even an alley.

by Toti O'Brien

My Father's Scream

"The only time I got worried," she says, "is when during the wake I heard your father yell. That long animal howl really scared me."

She is the family friend who is also a physician, sure to stick around during the funeral, Diazepam in her purse, alert, ready to deliver instructions, call an ambulance.

The old folks need watching, of course. An uncle has fainted as soon as he has arrived to church. He hasn't even made it to the pew, hastily shoved inside a taxi, brought home.

Luckily, no further incidents plague the ceremony.

"I was truly alarmed," she insists, "when he suddenly bent—hands grasping the rail, knees buckling below him—and let out that wild wail, unstoppable."

"You should take traditions into account," I add to mitigate her reaction, dull her shock. "Screaming before the dead is part of our southern lifestyle."

I remember Dad's mom at her husband's burials. She, always modest, shy, buttoned up, made quite a display. Yelling like a slaughtered swine, she attempted to throw herself inside the open hole where the coffin had been lowered, not yet covered with dirt. Of course she was held back, but she managed to engage in a furious struggle with those trying to contain her, in a sudden explosion of rage and despair.

But I don't describe such gruesome scene to the family doctor. No need.

She dismisses, anyway, my hypothesis of cultural influences over Father's manifestation of grief. Local habits, she affirms, cannot explain it, not so far, in such a different context. Does she mean 'in absence of witnesses able to correctly appreciate'? Perhaps.

Perhaps she is right. I don't know because I wasn't present. Didn't hear Father's scream.

I can hear it now, in my imagination. Very distinctly.

I can tell (could tell even the doctor) how it felt, because it echoes mine. The abrupt, ugly sound I uttered when the mournful news reached me on the phone.

I recall the cell on my bed, where it slipped from my hand as I slipped somewhere lower, not sure where. On the floor, I guess. I remember banging at the mattress—open palms? closed fists?—my arms groping in search of support or resistance, as my Dad's reached for the wooden rail.

I remember an unarticulated lament, awful. A long, indistinct vowel.

"He yelled like an animal," our doctor friend comments. She loves beasts. Her tone is compassionate, sympathetic. Like an animal, though the incomprehensible verse has a rather exact significance. It means 'no'. The most useless of words. The most helpless.

It means 'no' when we know that such syllable won't change a thing, yet everything should be changed. It means the kind of 'no' claiming to subvert the progress of time, to upset natural laws.

I'm not sure if such utterance of sheer revolt can be defined animal. Surely it isn't godly. I suspect it to be quintessentially human.

by Toti O'Brien

My Father's Scream - First published in *The Write Place At The Write Time*, Winter/Spring 2018

Getting lost is scary

We went to Thrifty. One second, we were in the same aisle, shopping. Something on the bottom shelf caught my attention. When I turned around, I did not see my mother. I ran down the aisle. Frantic, I searched the next aisle. She disappeared. One employee led me to the front of the store. They helped me sit on the checkout stand.

A girl cashier gave me a bag of marbles to make me feel better. The manager alerted shoppers over the PA system, "There is a little boy. He is looking for a lost mother."

My mother came. She put me down next to her. Then, walked away at a fast pace, with a tight grip on my left hand. I held the bag of marbles in my right hand. The marbles helped. It was even better to be found. No longer a lost little boy.

Getting lost is scary. One of the scariest experiences for a child. It is funny how children like to talk about scary things.

"Which monster is the scariest?" we asked each other in elementary school. My friends named one of the Universal Studios monsters. Frankenstein, the Mummy, the Wolf Man, Count Dracula, the Invisible Man, and others. We liked *Abbott and Costello Meet Frankenstein* (1948). Bud Abbott and Lou Costello made us laugh. And the movie had three monsters! Frankenstein, the Wolf Man, and Count Dracula.

I remember two television shows: *The Addams Family* and *The Munsters*. (Both series premiered in September 1964.) Two "monster-blended" families. They acted like our relatives, except they wore different makeup and clothes. So, all our childhood monsters were silly, not scary?

One of my college roommates was Wesley. He said, "The scariest movie was *Night of the Lepus*. Those mutated rabbits terrified me!" He described his anxiety while watching the 1972 American science fiction horror film.

"You know scientists make mistakes," he said.

"No way!" I said. "Even if rabbits were ten-feet tall! How would they develop a taste for human flesh?"

"I do not know. But it can happen," answered Wesley.

Wesley let his imagination get the best of him. One time, I studied late into the night. Wesley was sound asleep. He sat up in bed, faced in my direction, and screamed, "No! No! Not Luca Brasi!" Luca Brasi was Don Vito Corleone's most trusted enforcer in *The Godfather*. Wesley's eyes flashed with terror. He appeared like he was face-to-face with death. I underestimated the threat of killer rabbits and hitmen. But it could happen.

In recent years, my mother has struggled with dementia. She has "disappeared" again. Often, she gets confused about what to do next. Even more than forgetting names and words. We all have that experience. For her, reality became distorted. I remember a discussion about "Breakfast at 7:30 AM" at the senior home. It went on for several minutes. She said different times and different meals. The frustration in her voice grew. She asked me, "What do they do at your place?" She thought I lived in a senior home. Has she forgotten that people live in their own homes? What does she remember about her past life?

Several people helped my mother in her apartment. "Someone keeps stealing my things!" she told me.

"What are you missing?" I asked.

"My credit cards!" she complained.

We had similar conversations over the years. Many times, I found the "stolen" articles in the recesses of her room. They were so well hidden. She did not find them. Or, she forgot where she put them. I discovered the "stolen" credit card in the bottom of her desk drawer after the new one arrived. A few things are still missing. Her anxiety reminded me of Wesley. Theft by workers and death by killer rabbit or mafia hitman were unlikely. But it could happen.

My mother is lost. Where is she? What is she experiencing? I cannot imagine. Can a bag of marbles reach the lost one? Marbles meaning more than round glass with sparkles inside. Imagine marbles of memories. It would be nice.

Getting lost is scary. One of the scariest experiences for us.

by Dean Okamura

The Imaginary Ring

Where sweating men in tights and mismatched colors come at me, masks hiding their spinning eyes. Clerks, drivers, and men in suits assume their rough roles in the gallery of honor. See the tiny fight the large, left pummel right, the broken road, the jagged brawl, *Las Luchas.*

On the Metro I stand, hating. I resent eyes that will not meet me. I am willing to be kidnapped, even hung by my ankles from an electric grid if only someone will say, *Forgive me, but I know you.*

Mind if I arouse your bag? I ask a stranger. *That's mine,* snaps a voice from behind. *It's safe with me,* I say, *As long as you don't turn your back.* His pock-marked head swivels. I have stepped through the mist and feel so alive. The train has no sound. His skull narrows, his chin snaps like a gopher trap. I can smell his skin. I dance about the ring. I think I've won.

You don't know these people, my Aunt Eunice says at Thanksgiving. *I never hurt anybody,* I say. She taps her forehead, *The markings in your skull. Things have roosted there and left their rubbish spread about.* She takes a scoop of turkey stuffing. I would like to put it all to rest.

by Bill Ratner

The Heavens Weep for Us

They close ranks quickly, gray, pregnant banks of clouds rolling high above our heads. The wind waves wispy fingers behind trees, atop hills, in blue valleys and ridges, through crevices and slopes. Creeks puff their little bosoms and prepare to fill. God's little orchestra, syncopated, humming, thrumming, building, swelling till tears spill.

Black umbrellas clump together, edges wavy with dotted water. Neighbors and brothers and sisters and fathers and mothers meld in common pain. Both caskets are small, mere plain boxes hobbled together with moans and prayers and whys. Side by side, they could've been toy chests brimming with button-eye bears and dolls. They sit on dirt, bare pine boards streaked brown with rivulets of rain.

It's one wound in the earth, just one gape waiting patiently to be filled. One wound smaller than the usual, ashamed to swallow tiny coffins, preferring to be sated with a ripe old soul. But the baby caskets swinging on ropes slowly settle on the bottom, clicking on rocks and dusty stones, the two boxes touching sides, lying together, ready to be tucked in.

Stars fallen.

Moonbeams shamed.

Thunder should have alarmed the town: "Here, here, over here! Hear, hear!"

But the heavens were silent that night.

Silence same as silence old. Silence of the years, of neighbors choosing silence over truth, uncles choosing silence over courage, cousins choosing silence over conflict. Little children of the broken bones, tiny faces of the bloodied lips, slender shoulders with holes burnt in. Little children of the dirt. Little children blued and purpled, reddened and bumpy.

Little silent children in a silent watching town.

Flames licked the moon that night. Smoke curled into misty darkness too ashamed to swallow it. Wood crackled and heaved and buckled and smothered hope. Two swaddled lumps in the corner, under their mattress, clinging together, calling.

Does it matter that their mother was frightened of him? Torn by his knuckles, hands large and heavy like iron, frightened of his whiskey-breath and wide leather belt? Does it matter that she left that night?

Does it matter he survived? Clinking glasses at the tavern, readying his hands for her at home, licking sodden lips while flames licked his sons. And their mother not there, not knowing. Fickle moon not telling.

Stars fallen.

Moonbeams shamed.

But the heavens weep today, tears late, tears slow, silence interred.

The heavens weep for us.

by Thelma T. Reyna

Originally published in a prior version in the author's book, *The Heavens Weep for Us and Other Stories* (Outskirts Press, 2009).

Moment*

They say you know. Heart or brain or both are still, and your life's been scrubbed offline. Stripped, erased, gone blank. You've been unplugged, pulled back from calendars and clocks.

But scientists say humans know the moment they expire.

How did you feel, my love, when your heart screeched to a halt, one second to the next, stopped on a dime, as soon as anesthesia emptied in your veins? Just minor surgery, we'd been told. Just a little nick in the arm to implant this little device, we'd been told before they wheeled you into that room. But your heart went dead. Did you see the doctor's eyes glued to the screen, line flat and straight, humming not beeping? Did you see your surgeon toss his scalpel on the tray after slicing just a nick, hear him gasping, eyes wide?

They say humans know the moment they expire. They don't fully die for, perhaps, another hour.

Did you see their paddles shocking you, the tube they shoved into your throat, scrambling like bumblebees to start you up again? Did you see them press their palms upon your breast, pushing, pumping, sweating, taking turns and knowing you might be gone? What did they say? Which doctor ran the show? Did anyone exclaim, "Oh no! Oh no!" because it all happened at lightning speed?

They say humans know the moment they expire. They say the brain is still aware.

Did you hear your surgeon say, "I've got to tell his wife." Did you see him pull his face mask off, and did he scurry out the door, a frightened ant? They said compressions on your silent chest went on and on, that your heartbeat blipped back for a tiny flash, then disappeared, fading faster each time. Did you see them staring at the screen, and did anybody cry?

They say humans know the moment they expire.

Did you know I stood outside your room, behind the crowd, when they took me to your ICU? Did you see me standing tiptoed, face like stone, lips trembling as the medical team took turns climbing on a padded stool to press your chest nonstop? Did you see my praying lips, my stoic face awash in fear and hope, though doctors, nurses, medics, techs tired and slowed and shuffled limp-armed out your room?

They say humans know the moment they expire.

How did you feel, my love, to know you left without goodbyes, without a clue you'd not return to us? Did you see me press my face to the tall glass of the darkened wall outside your ICU, not bearing the sight of nurses removing blood and bandages, wiping your still body so I could come into the room to be alone with you?

They say humans know the moment they expire.

Did you see me climb into your bed once nurses left, and did you feel my arms tight across your chest and feel the wetness on your breast? Did you hear me telling you my grief, feel my fingers tracing tubes still bandaged to your arm, the arm they barely cut before your heart sank swiftly into silence? Did you feel my lips on yours?

So much to see, so much to hear when your moment of departure hits. Our loved ones who rushed over when I phoned, each of us hanging on to one another in disbelief. The nurse who brought us water and napkins and fruit to spell us through. Our chairs scraping the floor as we circled your bed and reached out to touch your hands and face, as if we could will you back to life.

by Thelma T. Reyna

Inspired by an article "Scientists Find That Humans Actually Know When They Have Died." Based on research by Dr. Sam Parnia. In braincharm. com/2018/11/27/

Originally published in the author's book, *Dearest Papa: A Memoir in Poems* (Golden Foothills Press, 2020).

Mysteries, I

Only a potato, dusty ball of lifeless starch: humble thing, even if it fits as if made for the hand. But this lumpen nightshade is a wonder—is Lazarus! You do not need, even, to pray, only to leave it in a dry place and forget, or have patience, and leave it be. It will become as alien as a creature from the bottom of the sea, dimpled eyes budding into pink, purple, bergamot anemones, this thing that was a rotten stone in your hand! The tender and unassuming French Fingerling can do this every bit as well as the beloved Yukon Gold or the bold heirloom Purple Peruvian: left alone for a week, in a scant six inches of dirt, the small coral monsters have sent up tightly furled periscopes, pushing the soil bodily aside in their need for the sky. Daily now—in the space of one warm afternoon—there are leaves and more leaves, curled and coiling faster than you can count them, dusty with fur, eager viridian, even indigo toward the base; a stem, becoming a stalk, pushing up and up and up— Bury half this young miracle alive, before it is even one foot high. It will take more than three days, but, interred in the dry, soft earth, instead of worms and rot potatoes accrete, and wait in the rich dark for their leaves to wither and be unearthed.

by Lauren Tyler-Rickon

Going To Church

We sat in front of the four-foot tall, shiny mahogany and oak Motorola radio looking up as if we could see the voices coming out of the brown grill-cloth covering the speaker. In those days crossing our legs on the floor for a half an hour didn't hurt, and when we heard the feint call outside we knew the ragman was snapping the reins of that slow moving horse as he called out in his loud clear voice as if in song, "Any ra-a-a-a-a-a-a-gs toda-a--a-ay, any ra-a-a-ags toda-a-a-ay," and the three of us leaped to our feet forgetting about the weekly radio show, now running full speed across the dining room, through the kitchen, over the linoleum, out the back door.

Jimmy had the lead, Michael second and I trailed in a streak reinforcing the order of our childhood society: the oldest, the middle, the youngest. We hit the big wooden gate in that order just as the ragman rounded the corner into our alley. Black square blinders covered the eyes of the old chestnut horse as it shuffled its way up the alley, kicking up dust clouds, we running toward it, our six brown legs scrambling. We pull alongside the sun faded wooden cart and scream to the old rag man like a call and response, his "Any rags today," then our "Any balls today, Any balls today, any balls today?" This is our fevered litany, Any Bal-l-l-l-l-s today?

Our high-pitched prayer played against his fine tenor, "Any ra-a-a-ags tod-a-a-ay." Then the miracle happens—as it always happens, with barely a movement from his body, the wrist flicking like a fine tuned instrument, small weathered tennis balls leave his tan withered hands. They float through the blue sky, small and tattered against the sun. Our manna comes tumbling down, small arms outstretched and we are squealing in delight, our young bodies twisted in rapture as we reach, jump and lunge for a clean catch, some bouncing off of us and then it is over and we run, stoop, grab the round gifts. Some in bounce, some at roll, nothing else exists except this moment, the clicking of the hooves, a staccato neigh, the pure tenor ring, "Any ra-a--ags toda-a-ay" growing fainter and fainter but still mixing with the soprano chorus of laughter and short giggles of our pure

ecstasy.

by R.S. Rocha

Bios

Jessica Abughattas is an American poet of Palestinian heritage. Her debut book, Strip, won the Etel Adnan Poetry Prize and will be published by University of Arkansas in 2020. She is a Kundiman fellow and a graduate of the Antioch University Los Angeles MFA in Creative Writing program. Her poems appear in Waxwing, The Journal, Redivider, and elsewhere. Best, Jessica Abughattas 2045 El Molino Avenue Altadena, CA 91001 jabughattas@antioch.edu 818.808.8229

Micaela Accardi-Krown is an emerging author in the Los Angeles area and has been a proud resident of Altadena for 18 years. Her writing often deals with childhood, loss, grief, the moments in between, and are always set in worlds similar to ours, but with a bit more magic.

Vibiana Aparicio-Chamberlin is currently working on a novel about the Yaqui Indians in early 19th Century Sonora. She is also the author and illustrator of internationally awarded *Mi Amor, A Memoir*. Vibiana has earned Masters Degrees in the areas of Creative Writing, Theater Arts and in Educational Administration. She was born in Boyle Heights, East Los Angeles and is an artist-author who is an accomplished poet, painter, novelist, and professor of art, and creative writing. Her recent exhibitions and lectures were at UC Santa Barbara, at Cal State Channel Islands and at the Vincent Price Museum, as a Getty artist for Pacific Standard Times. Vibiana has lived in Pasadena since 1964 and is a political activist for Chicano Latino struggles.

Gloria Arellanes was born in East Los Angeles in 1946, her father was a first-generation Mexican-American and her mother was Tongva.

In 1967, Arellanes joined the Brown Berets. Serving as the Minister of Finance and Correspondence of the Brown Berets's founding chapter in Los

Angeles, she was the only woman to hold a major leadership position. The Berets worked to achieve better education for Chicano youth, end police brutality against minorities, and promote cultural pride. They also worked on building community programs, the first of which was the Barrio Free Clinic, which Arellanes was given the responsibility of coordinating. In 1969, she was made the official clinic director.

Following her time with the Berets, Arellanes has reconnected with her Native American heritage and is now an elder of the Tongva tribe. She served as a secretary on the Tribal Council and is part of an Indigenous Grandmothers group.

Beth Baird Poetry is an integral part of all my endeavors. I am a songwriter, a story teller, and a singer. I love spoken word, music, and theater. I have written more than 30 songs and countless poems. My poems have been published twice in Serbia and I was invited to Belgrade to read at the International Writer's Meeting. I have read my poetry on local tv and throughout Europe. I live in Altadena.

Judy Barrat has been a writer of poetry and fiction most of her life as a hobby and began presenting her work publicly in Los Angeles several years ago at open readings, as well as at music venues, sometimes with a vocalist weaving a song around one of her poems. She has been a featured poet at several Los Angeles poetry venues and has performed three very well reviewed one-woman shows of her poetry and stories, with musical accompaniment, at The Gardenia Club in Hollywood. Her work has been published in several anthologies, magazines and on-line journals

Lynne Bronstein is a widely published poet, fiction writer, and journalist and has been nominated twice for the Pushcart Prize and three times for the Best of the Net anthology. She also acts with the Hollywood Legacy Players and performs in storytelling shows. Her short story "The Magic Candles" was read on National Public Radio. She lives in the San Fernando Valley.

Jeffrey Bryant I am a writer and poet living in Los Angeles. My work has appeared in the L.A. Weekly, L.A. Times, Poetic Diversity and in the anthology Coiled Serpent from Tia Chucha Press.

Tommy Vinh Bui putters around town scribbling notes on his palm and attempts to decipher the sweaty blotches later into poetry. The results are more misses than hits. But he'll keep earnestly endeavouring to become proficient and perfect his palm-poetry technique. He recently discovered he's NOT allergic to peanuts.

Tim Callahan worked for many years as an artist in the animation industry. He began seriously writing poetry in 2011. He lives with his wife, Bon, in the foothills of Altadena in close company with deer, coyotes, bobcats and bears.

Don Kingfisher Campbell, MFA in Creative Writing from Antioch University Los Angeles, has taught Writers Seminar at Occidental College Upward Bound for 35 years, been a coach and judge for Poetry Out Loud, a performing poet/teacher for Red Hen Press Youth Writing Workshops, Los Angeles Area Coordinator and Board Member of California Poets In The Schools, poetry editor of the Angel City Review, publisher of Spectrum and the San Gabriel Valley Poetry Quarterly, leader of the Emerging Urban Poets writing and Deep Critique workshops, organizer of the San Gabriel Valley Poetry Festival, and host of the Saturday Afternoon Poetry reading series in Pasadena, California. For awards, features, and publication credits, please go to: http://dkc1031.blogspot.com

Christine Candland My poems have been included in the Altadena Poetry Review 2018 and 2019. I have read my poems at the Brentwood, Mar Vista and Whittier Libraries. I have participated on a writing panel at Santa Monica College. I have published two novels Topaz Woman and Pleiades Rising. Both have won awards. I write poetry to express the beauty around me in human behavior and nature.

Peggy Castro I am retired peer partner who worked with the homeless. I divide my time between Tacoma and Southern California to be with my family. I feel particularly blessed to have the love of my family and friends. I have my sanity and although I do not have a master or dogma I have confidence in my spirituality. I feel very grateful to be able to create and enjoy the beauty of this world. Impermanence does not bother me. Not knowing does not bother me. Gratitude sums it up.

Chuka Susan Chesney I am an artist, a sculptor, and a published poet. My work is represented by Aarnun Gallery in Pasadena. I grew up and reside in the Los Angeles area. My paintings and drawings are heavily influenced by the Latin culture. For many years, I kept it a secret that I love to write poetry, especially in the middle of the night. I kept my poems in a drawer in my desk and didn't show them to anyone except my family. A couple of years ago, I started submitting them, and a few of them have been published.

Philip Chiao Writing poetry has been a process of self discovery - an investigation of the self, the people and the world around me, and the language I can use to communicate my findings. Since English is my second language, I am particularly sensitive in finding economic ways to construct poems within my limited language skills. I am also very much aware of my background as a first generation American - first arriving US by way of North Africa, Europe and my birth place, Taiwan. My personal perspective has been very much enriched by the variety of living experiences around different parts of the world.

Jackie Chou is a neurodivergent poet who writes poetry to satisfy her obsessive-compulsive need to capture thoughts, feelings, and images before they slip away from her consciousness. She feels a sense of loss and inadequacy both as a poet and a human being when she fails to do so. She uses poetry to make meaning out of fragile and ephemeral experiences. Her work has been published in the Journal of Modern Poetry 21 Dear Mr.

President anthology, Creative Talents Unleashed anthologies, and others. She was nominated for a Best of the Net in 2018 by Hidden Constellation.

Teresa Mei Chuc Poet Laureate of Altadena (2018 to 2020), Teresa Mei Chuc is the author of three full-length collections of poetry, *Red Thread* (Fithian Press, 2012), *Keeper of the Winds* (FootHills Publishing, 2014) and *Invisible Light* (Many Voices Press, 2018). She was born in Saigon, Vietnam and immigrated to the U.S. under political asylum with her mother and brother shortly after the Vietnam War while her father remained in a Vietcong "reeducation" camp for nine years. Her poetry appears in journals such as *Consequence Magazine, EarthSpeak Magazine, Hawai'i Pacific Review, Kyoto Journal, Poet Lore, Rattle, Whitefish Review, Verse Daily* and in anthologies such as *New Poets of the American West* (Many Voices Press, 2010), *With Our Eyes Wide Open: Poems of the New American Century* (West End Press, 2014, and *Inheriting the War: Poetry and Prose by Descendants of Vietnam Veterans and Refugees* (W.W. Norton, 2017). Teresa is a graduate of the Masters in Fine Arts in Creative Writing program at Goddard College in Plainfield, Vermont and teaches literature and writing at a public high school in Los Angeles.

Marsha Cifarelli I m a long time teacher and parent. I'm a grandmother. From children and people with limited English, I have learned to express a great deal with minimum words. It's not always easy.

Reg Clarkinia is a queer writer, artist and astrologer. They have created several comedy shows including the noir sketch comedy series, NIGHT PLANE; the kid-led children's show, BART TRAIN KITTIES; and LORD FRY, a solo character show, performed at Sweeny-Kaye Gallery in Oakland, CA. Reg was an artist in residence at Thank You For Coming for their divination deck based on astrology archetypes. Their poetry is about healing in everyday spaces, neighborhoods, ancestors, transformation and queerness. You can find Reg's poems, essays and astrology writings at QUEERAUNTIE.com.

Coco Author of Unicorn Psychosis is a Pasadena resident and Mental Health Awareness Advocate. Writing poetry, children's literature and other literary works has been a secret passion since childhood. Born into a life of medical impossibilities, numerous traumas, and abuse writing provided strength and endurance to carry on. Mother of two boys which was deemed medically impossible due to the nature of the vast medical conditions sustained throughout life. Given a life expectancy of 18 armed with determination now over 40 and fiercely fighting the day to day traumas of life through verse.

Lisbeth Coiman is a bilingual writer from Venezuela, standing on a blurred line between mental health and immigration. Coiman's work has been appeared in Entropy, Nailed, The Literary Kitchen, and Rabid Oaks, among other online magazines and journals. Her self-published book, I Asked the Blue Heron: A Memoir, 2017, explores the intersection between mental illness and immigration, celebrates friendship, and draws attention to child abuse. Coiman is an active member of Women Who Submit - Los Angeles. She teaches English as a Second Language to adult students in Los Angeles. She dances salsa to beat depression.

Stephen Colley is a retired software engineer/manager who's been writing poems for 30+ years – always metered, almost always rhymed, typically sonnets or triple limericks. He's also written three screenplays and a good deal of classical music, including a song cycle on Lord of the Rings poems and settings of 15 Robert Frost poems.

Chris Cressey recently moved to the Pasadena area after 40 years in Malibu. She enjoys outdoor activities and being close to her grand daughter. Writing has become a welcome means of self expression. She has been published in The Nasty Woman's Almanac and Spectrum.

Pat Cross A sometimes poet, sometimes musician and a full-time retired teacher who still finds things to teach people.

Bill Cushing lived in various states and the Caribbean before moving to Glendale, where he resides with his wife and their son. He was called the "blue collar" poet by classmates at Central Florida because of his years in the Navy and later as an electrician on oil tankers, naval vessels, and fishing boats before returning to college, later earning an MFA in writing from Vermont's Goddard College. Bill's poetry has appeared in numerous journals, both in print and online, including both volumes of the award-winning Stories of Music. In 2019, he won Spectrum's San Gabriel Valley chapbook competition.

Triniti Daniel-Robinson I am 19 years old currently completing my second semester at the University of Southern California and I'm majoring in Comparative Literature. I moved to Palmdale in 2011 from LA but still commuted to LA for school all the way through high school. I started writing poetry in 9th grade and competed in NAACP's Beverly Hills ACTSO branch all 4 years in high school but never placed while at nationals in my category Written Poetry. I really enjoy writing poetry and plan to publish a book of poetry one day.

Stacy DeGroot is a visual design and word artist living in the Arts District of DTLA with her two young daughters. A native of Los Angeles with an MFA in Creative Writing, her poetry appears in several online and print publications. While poetry is at the heart of all of her artistic pursuits, it is the poetic image, in all of its creative expressions, which both captures and frees her spirit.

Valena Dismukes Formerly from St. Louis. Missouri, I found my home in Los Angeles in 1960, teaching junior and senior high school and working as a mentor teacher. During that time, I also developed an interest in photography and writing and have published several books based upon those interests. My most notable book was "The Red-Black Connection" about people of African and American Indian heritage.

Tiffany Do goes by TiDo and use she/her pronouns. I'm growing into teaching as a career and community organizing with Chinatown Community for Equitable Development (CCED) and Free Radicals. Relationship building is not the only thing that nourishes my being, so does flatulent humor, dirt, plants, doggos, hikes, books, poetry and so many other things.

Mel Donalson is a poet, fiction writer, and playwright. His most recent novel is the contemporary drama, entitled The Third Woman.

Megan Dorame is a Tongva poet who lives and writes in Santa Ana, California. She holds a BA in anthropology from the University of Oklahoma, and works to reclaim and revitalize the Tongva language. Megan is a 2020 PEN Emerging Voices Fellow and her work has appeared in *The Ear, Dryland*, and *The Offing*, among others. Megan is working on a collection of poems inspired by the complicated history of her people.

Linda Dove holds a Ph.D. in Renaissance literature and teaches college writing. She is also an award-winning poet of four books: In Defense of Objects (2009), O Dear Deer, (2011), This Too (2017), and Fearn (2019), as well as the scholarly collection of essays, Women, Writing, and the Reproduction of Culture in Tudor and Stuart Britain (2000). Poems have been nominated for a Pushcart Prize, the Robert H. Winner Award from the Poetry Society of America, Best of the Net, and Best Microfiction. She lives with her human family, two Jack Russell terriers, and two backyard chickens in the foothills east of Los Angeles, and she serves as the faculty editor of MORIA Literary Magazine at Woodbury University in Burbank.

Pauline Dutton As a teen I wrote poetry to express my angst. Years later, a friend who had seen my autobiographical writing, told me I was a poet and invited me to a workshop. I knew little about technique but enjoyed the comradery and learning as I muddled along. It's thrilling to tap into the "other," to be surprised by what appears. There's also the inspiring fun of listening to poets read their work and perform my own. In short, poetry makes my life joyful and adds meaning to everything.

Richard Dutton Earlier in my career I did some technical writing and presentations. In retirement from engineering and education with three post grad degrees, Writing poetry and critiquing help me clarify my emotional memories and current thinking. I also enjoy reading my poetry aloud due to some early acting and orating. I first got into poetry because my wife started going to poetry workshops and I like doing things with her. As I continued learning about poetry I came to enjoy the various challenges of writing, the fun of wordplay, and the comradery of other poets.

Alicia Elkort's poetry has been published in AGNI, Arsenic Lobster, Black Lawrence Press, Georgia Review, Heron Tree, The Hunger Journal, Jet Fuel Review, Menacing Hedge, Rogue Agent, Stirring: A Literary Collection, Tinderbox Poetry Journal, as well as many others. Her poems have been nominated for the Orisons Anthology (2016), the Pushcart (2017), and A Best of the Net (2018). Alicia reads for Tinderbox Poetry Journal, mostly with a cup of strong black tea in hand.

Dawn Robin English I was born to turn my hardships into something creative and in doing so hopefully help or inspire others to be honest and share their stories with others...no matter how dark. In addition to poetry, my memoirs and fiction, I hope to get back into my singing and song writing in the very near future.

Lynn Fang I am a soil and compost specialist working on building community composting and urban farming infrastructure in LA County. I teach, speak, and consult on soil, compost, and ecological design. I am also a writer and artist inspired by the magic of soil, plants, flowers, and mushrooms.

Lynn Fayne Resident of Altadena, Ca. where I write poems and paint paintings.

Emily Fernandez teaches at Pasadena City College, and lives in El Sereno. Her chapbook, Procession of Martyrs, was published in 2018 by Finishing Line Press.

Mark A. Fisher is a writer, poet, and playwright living in Tehachapi, CA. His poetry has appeared in: A Sharp Piece of Awesome, Dragon Poet Review, Penumbra, Elegant Rage: A Poetic Tribute to Woody Guthrie, and many other places. His first chapbook, drifter, is available from Amazon. His second, hour of lead, won the 2017 San Gabriel Valley Poetry Chapbook contest. His plays have appeared on California stages in Pine Mountain Club, Tehachapi, Bakersfield, and Hayward. He was nominated for a Pushcart Prize in 2015 for his poem "papyrus" in the Altadena Poetry Review. He has also won cooking ribbons at the Kern County Fair.

Oombi Solis Flores Mexican born, Oombi Solis Flores, is a queer/non-binary poet living in the Northeast San Fernando Valley. Their poems explores queer existence, and love in its endless forms. They have been featured in *Razorcake Issue* #102, and *Sister Spit: QTPOC Cruising the West Tour*. Contact them: instagram @jotitadeamor dearjotitadeamor@gmail.com

Katherine Footracer lives in Altadena with her sweetie, dogs, and native garden. She volunteers with Eaton Canyon Nature Center and works as a physician assistant. She loves the beauty of California, of friends, and of words.

GT Foster A native Californian, Vietnam War veteran, retired educator, and grandfather, my first published poem, written in the aftermath of the Eric Garner killing appeared in the Pasadena Weekly in 2015 after taking my frustration out on blank pages and then to the newspaper. Have since been nominated for a 2017 Pushcart, become co-host of Saturday Afternoon Poetry and general manager of SPECTRUM, now an international poetry quarterly having published poets from France and Plumstead, London, U.K.

Joyce Futa has lived in Altadena since 2012. Previously, she was a San Franciscan for 50 years. Her poetry book "Lit Windows: A Book of Haibun and Tanka Prose" was published in 2017 by Blue Light Press.

Martina R. Gallegos Martina came from Mexico and attended Pasadena High school, Oxnard College, CSUN. She got a Master's from Gran Canyon University after a massive stroke. She published her first book in 2016. Her poems appeared in Hometown Pasadena, Silver Birch Press, Altadena Poetry Review: Anthology 2015, Lummox, Poets Responding to SB1070, and Basta! She was named one of Altadena Poetry Review: Anthology 2017, and San Gabriel Valley Quarterly top poets.

Jerry Garcia spent his childhood fearing "the bomb" and was a teenager during the "Summer of Love." He studied Communication Arts at Loyola Marymount University during the Watergate Era becoming a film editor and producer of television commercials, documentaries and motion picture previews. His poetry has been seen in various journals and anthologies, including "Wide Awake: Poets of Los Angeles and Beyond," "Coiled Serpent Anthology," "Voices from Leimert Park Redux," "The San Pedro River Review," "Dark Ink Anthology," "The Chiron Review," and "Askew Magazine." He has two books of poetry, the full-length collection On Summer Solstice Road (2016 Green Tara Press) and a chapbook Hitchhiking With the Guilty (2010 GND Press). Jerry lives in the San Fernando Valley with his wife Becky and their poetic dog Japhy Ryder.

Catherine Gewertz has been a cocktail waitress, garage band singer, pie baker, and typewriter poet-for-hire. To earn a steady living, though, she's a newspaper reporter. She loves a nice turn around the two-step floor, and a glass of Bourbon, neat. Her work appears in *True Chili* and *Raw Art Review*.

Luz Gutierrez I am 21 year old UCLA student. I've always loved history, law and politics but poetry is my new love. My philosophy is: adventure on the page and in life.

Charles Harmon Loves to write, loves to live, loves to love, loves to cook, loves to eat. Teaching science is like cooking, cooking is like writing poetry, poetry is about life, love is about living and living is being in love. Long live poetry, life, and love! Enjoys cooking for his family and friends, writing poetry and stories and songs. Currently working on a novel.

Shirley Harris I'm a retired professional with a passion for writing. I've had this passion since childhood and I've pursued it intermittently throughout my life. I write for pleasure, out of pain and sometimes out of a simple desire to record my thoughts and feelings for posterity.

Hazel Clayton Harrison believes that poetry and storytelling have the power to transform the world. She is the 2018-2020 Altadena Poet Laureate, Community Events. For her writing is a healing balm for the soul. She is a member of the Pasadena Rose Poets, an ensemble that shares their poetry in unexpected places, such as at local City Council meetings. Her works have been published in *Grandfathers, Altadena Poetry Review Anthology 2015—2019, Coiled Serpent, Journal of Modern Poetry 20 & 21*, and other anthologies. She is the author of *The Story of Christmas Tree Lane.* Her memoir, *Crossing the River Ohio*, and her latest collection of poetry and prose, *Down Freedom Road*, are available on Amazon.com.

Eleanor Harvey is a teenage poetess who lives in Altadena. Her poems have been recognized by Forward Arts and the Scholastic Arts and Writing Awards.

Teri Hicks I am only that I am. Credentialed by The Creator of all that is. Thoughts culled from the Universal Mind, words borrowed from books, teachers, conversations heard in passing, dreams, memories from past lives, beliefs harvested from day to day experiences. As the dusk of my life approaches, I pen what Creator gifts to me as a testament that I am here, I exist, I live, I love, I am. Teri Hicks

Andria Hill From pen to paper, voice; a haven in trees. Andria Hill, poet, artist, singer, writes to heal, to hope, to feel, to cope. To remember.

Randel Horton is the author of Sounds of Poetry, The Sample Sad Collection, which expresses spirituality, life, death, love, hate, anger, and happiness all in a few pages of words. He also co-arranged and produced the CD, New Times, a mix of original poetry and smooth jazz. His work is published in Nobel House Anthology, Theater of the Mind, and in many other anthologies.

Gerda Govine Ituarte is the author of four poetry collections and the Editor of the Pasadena Rose Poets Collection 2019. In February 2017 poetry readings were initiated at Pasadena City Council Meetings, which continues. Book five is a work-in-progress. Her poems were published in Coiled Serpent, Journal of Modern Poetry, Altadena Poetry Review, Ms Aligned 1-3, Dryland Arts and Letters and The New Engagement. Govine Ituarte read and exhibited at galleries, museums and cultural centers in Los Angeles and San Diego and in Canada, Colombia, Cuba, Mexico and the UK. She has an Ed.D. from Teachers College, Columbia University.

Ellice Jeon I published my two poetry books so far. They both were written in Korean. In this November a few of my poems were selected and would be published as a electronic books by 'Dizibooks' company in Korea. As I write my poetry, I became to like sharing my thoughts with my children and my grandchildren who were born in the US. And Mr. Craig Cotter who I met at PCC in a Poetry workshop and helped me a lot in grammar and stuff. Now I am so excited to share my poems with all my poetry friends at 'Altadena Poetry Review' for the first time and ever.

Lois P. Jones is an award-winning poet residing in South Pasadena, California. Her poem Reflections on La Scapigliata was featured as a film adaptation for the 2019 Visible Poetry Project. In addition to her extensive publications, she was a winning finalist for the 2018 Terrain Poetry Contest judged by Jane Hirshfield, a recipient of the Lascaux Poetry Prize, the 2016 Bristol Poetry Prize and the 2012 Tiferet Poetry Prize. Her first collection Night Ladder listed for the Julie Suk and the Lascaux Poetry Awards. Lois hosts KPFK's Poets Café and is poetry editor of the Pushcart Prize winning Kyoto Journal.

Lorelei Kay is a mom, a grandmother, a writer, and a poet. Ever since her dad sat her down and helped her write her first poem, she was hooked. She attended Brigham Young University on a journalism scholarship. Lorelei's poems have appeared in anthologies, online publications, and magazines. She's also recently published her award-winning memoir, "From Mormon to Mermaid." Lorelei serves as vice president of the High Desert Chapter of The California Writer's Club, has served on the a Blue Ribbon Judging Panel for Scholastic Arts and Writing Awards, and as a mentor on the Dorothy C. Blakely Memoir Project.

Jan King I am one of two editors for the Stone Bird: an Eagle Rock Library Anthology. I have published in The Edgar Allan Poe Commemorative; The Southern California Haiku Society Athology, What the Wind Can't Touch; Timeless Voices Poetry Anthology; and in Bravo: A Magazine for Poets, The Altadena Poetry Review 2019, Poetry and Paint, Lummox and elsewhere. I believe that what we see creates what we feel, and that what we feel impels what we see.

Cybele Garcia Kohel - I am a poet living in Pasadena, California. Born in Puerto Rico, I write about life through the many lenses provided me by my diverse background, my Generation X upbringing, and the streets of Los Angeles. She is a cultural worker, community agitator and serious dog lover. You can read her poems in *Vine Leaves Journal* Issue #15 (2015), *These Fragile Lilacs Poetry Journal the Women's Voices Issue* (June 2017), *the Altadena Poetry Review* (2017, 2018), *New American Legends* (April, 2019) and the upcoming *Nightingale and Sparrow* (2020).

Deborah P Kolodji is the California regional coordinator for the Haiku Society of America and a member of the board of directors for Haiku North America. The former president of the Science Fiction Poetry Association, Kolodji is also is a member of the Southern California Haiku Study Group, the Haiku Poets of Northern California , the Yuki Teikei Haiku Society, Haiku Canada, and the California State Poetry Society. Her first full-length book of haiku and senryu, Highway of Sleeping Towns, from Shabda Press, was awarded a Touchstone Distinguished Book Award from The Haiku Foundation.

Linda Kraai holds a B.A. from Hanover College in Indiana and an M.A. from the University of Northern Colorado in Greeley. Throughout her thirty-two year teaching career, she wrote "occasional poems" to celebrate milestones in the lives of her family and friends. In retirement she attends the Osha Lifelong Learning Poetry for Pleasure class at California State University, Fullerton, and a weekly poetry workshop in Claremont. Her poems have been published in Altadena Poetry Review 2017, 2018, 2019, Spectrum 2018, and Osha Lifelong Learning California State University, Fullerton Poetry Anthology 2016, 2019.

Joan Krieger-Hoffman is a human. She is a partner at FRED HOFFMAN ARCHITECTURE Vice Chairman Mulholland Design Review Board appointed by LA City Council Ms.Hoffman received a "Women Who Mean Business Award" from the SFV Business Journal Hosted "A Woman's Point of View" A television program on the Cox Cable Network She has had a wonderful life ...so far

Tom Laichas's recent work has appeared or is forthcoming in Big Window Review, 3.1 Venice, Masque & Spectacle, Courtship of the Winds, and elsewhere. His first collection, Empire of Eden, is due out in 2020 from High Window Press (UK). He is currently at work on a new project, 300 Streets of Venice California.

Peter Larsen is a retired wood sculptor. One of the advantages of poetry over sculpture is that you can stare at a draft, take it for a hike, or ignore it for weeks and it still evolves. Wood sculpture just sits on your bench until you resume whacking at it.

Courtney Lavender is a native Los Angeleno with deep roots in Ireland. She plays with her band Xs & ARROWs and works in the music industry. Her poems have been published in Honest Ulsterman, Picaroon, Bangor Literary Journal, Fat Damsel, Live Encounters, Altadena Poetry Review, and she is working toward her first collection.

Sharmagne Leland-St. John, 14-time Pushcart Prize nominee, is a Native American poet, concert performer, lyricist, artist, filmmaker. and Editor-in-Chief of the poetry e-zine quillandparchment.com. Sharmagne spends time between her home in the Hollywood Hills, in CA, fly fishing lodge on the Stillaguamish River in the Pacific Norhtwest, hacienda in Taos, N.M and her Villetta in Tuscany. Her work can be found in anthologies as well as on-line. She has published 4 books collections of poetry, edited Cradle Songs: An Anthology of Poetry on Motherhood, winner of the International Book Award 2013 and co-authored Designing Movies: Portrait of a Hollywood Artist.

Nancy Lind is a retired professor of English Literature. She is a recent transplant from New York to Pasadena. In her retirement she has been active in literary clubs and poetry groups. She has had poems published in journals such as JOMP, 34th Parrallel, and Impulse. She was also a Pushcart nominee. Her Scandinavian heritage influences her writings.

Janis Lukstein loves to perform playful, rhyming and stream-of-consciousness poetry. She wears costumes enhancing her comedic and dramatic poems. Join her on the 3rd Saturday of the Month from 2-4 with the SoCalHaikuStudyGroup@yahoogroups.org of Pasadena at the Hill Ave.

Library. Consider subscribing to Yuki Teikei's instructional Geppo journal for more haiku info. She has started writing 5 line tanka and loves to be challenged by the Tanka Society of America's Tanka Café theme, plus wonderful Altadena's Poetry Review publication and program every April. CALKEYPALS@aol.com

Joseph Lusnia is a Husband, Father, Worker, Writer.

Radomir Vojtech Luza was born in 1963 in Vienna, Austria to renowned Czech parents the veteran SAG/AFTRA/AEA member of over 30 years has been the Poet Laureate of North Hollywood, CA for eight years and a Pushcart Prize Nominee. The author of 30 books (26 Collections of Poetry) published his most recent Tome in November of 2018. Titled "Sidewalks and Street Corners", the Poetry Collection was released by Christian Faith Publishing to rave reviews and stellar criticism. in the same year the long time stand-up comedian recorded "An Autumn Day in the Life of L.A. to staggering popularity and quiet notoriety. Luza has Featured his poetry over 100 times around the country. His work appears in nearly 90 literary journals, anthologies, websites and other media. Radomir has also hosted, organized and curated over a dozen poetry readings nation wide. Finally, the 2016 Irwin Award-Winner for "Most Creative Book of Poetry for "Eros of Angels" (2016) and Writers Digest and 2018 Highland Park Poetry Challenge Honorable Mention is the publisher and editor of the Literary Journal, "Voices in the Library" published by Red Doubloon Publishing, the literary arm of Radman Productions.

Roberta H Martínez was born and raised in East Los Angeles, California. She received her BA in Music and MA in Music History from UCR. Ms. Martínez has extensive experience as a musician. *Arcadia Publishing* set her book, <u>Latinos in Pasadena</u>, on the market in 2009. She has just completed her first three plays collected as the *Pan Dulce Trilogy*.

Deborah McGaffey Born in Los Angeles, I received my BA. in Philosophy from California State University, Fullerton, and my M.A. in Counseling Psychology from Pepperdine University. I published my first book of poetry at the age of 66, so it was later in life before I made a serious commitment to following my dreams. After spending over twenty years in the beautiful Pacific Northwest, I now reside back in Los Angeles where I enjoy pursuing my passion of writing and spending time with my now-grown children and my grandchildren.

Roshan Zoe Moazed graduated from Brown University in 2017, and now lives in Somerville, Massachusetts, where she works at a coffee shop she loves with all of her heart. When she isn't making coffee for the patrons of North Cambridge, you can find her sitting on the floor typing furiously on her laptop, working on her MFA applications, making homemade soap, and collecting things the color of sunset orange. She is excited to go to grad school in Fall 2020 and plans to write feverishly until then.

Penelope Moffet is a Southern California poet with work published in many literary journals and several anthologies. She also published two chapbooks: *Keeping Still* (Dorland Mountain Arts Colony, 1995) and *It Isn't That They Mean to Kill You* (Arroyo Seco Press, 2018).

Andrea Seferina Morales was born on May 20, 1977. Due to her father's exposure to Agent Orange in the Vietnam War, at 3 years old, she started dialysis treatments. Three days a week, she continued on dialysis up to her death. She did have a break from 24 years when she received a kidney and her mother, me (Petra Morales), was the donor.

Andrea was a spunky, fun girl always joking, laughing…I believe that's what kept her strong to be able to endure her dialysis treatments that would leave her drained. During the time she spent at the hospital up to her teen years, she was encouraged to write so she started to write many poems about her pets, family, friends.

I remember she would ask, "Mom, when I die will people remember me?" She would also ask, "What is my purpose in life?" And there were days that she would say, "Mom, I feel so happy!" I would tell her, "Hold on to those days filled with such peace and love."

Andrea passed on a special day for the Mexican/Mexicano/Chicano people – she passed on September 16th, El Dia Del Grito! Dia de la Indepencia, the revolt against the Spanish regime.

(Andrea Seferina Morales' bio was written by her mother, Petra Morales)

Alejandro Zapote Morales is a novelist and short story writer. His recent works include a novel *River of Angels* and *Little Nation*, a collection of short stories.

Toni Mosley is a former nonprofit executive who introduced creative writing to youngsters who struggled to read and write, Mosley is now a member of the Pasadena Rose Poets and is working on her memoir, *Dead Flies in the Window Sill*.

Elliott Lee Negrin is a young writer living in the greater San Gabriel Valley. As a young bisexual man, and a first generation American, Negrin has always been driven by adversity and hardship to challenge himself and the world around him with his writing.

Janet Nippell's poems have appeared in San Pedro River Review, Miramar, Askew, Tia Chucha's Coiled Serpent anthology, Rattle, A Narrow Fellow, Christianity & Literature, and in the Altadena Poetry Review. She and Ben

Yandell narrated some long walks, long ago, in Mostly on Foot, A Year in L.A. (Floating Island, 1989).

Christian Nuno When I find myself in the binds of my deepest depression I am overwhelmed with a desire to neither live nor die, but return to a collective entity to be reformed. Not a second chance as myself, but a chance for a new life to live, and hopefully endure.

Toti O'Brien is the Italian Accordionist with the Irish Last Name. She was born in Rome then moved to Los Angeles, where she makes a living as a self-employed artist, performing musician and professional dancer. Her work has most recently appeared in the anthology *Finding Light in Unexpected Places*, *Colorado Boulevard*, *Abstract Contemporary*, and *Mortar Magazine*.

Dean Okamura resides in Torrance, California.

Atlakatl Orozco is a humanimal experiment experiencing the human experience. artist. creative destroyer. mazahua/huichol/rarámuri. indigenous eagle and the condor baby. Young warrior and bookstore assistant of Tia Chucha's Bookstore & Centro Cultural, atlakatl ce tochtli. 20yrs old

Kelving Ortiz lives in Pacoima, Los Angeles CA. Poetry is something that helps her cope with the internal struggles of her "negative" emotions, like self-doubt, depression, and anger. Being involved with Luis J. Rodriguez out in Sylmar, going to open mics at Tia Chuchas, and becoming a part of the Young Warriors youth program since the age of eighteen, has made her fall in love with the arts and become a more spiritual individual. Thanks to community volunteer work, she has grown to love the aspects of my Central American culture.

Luis Ortiz Ever since I was diagnosed with cancer at the age of 16, I've never been the same. From that day on, I decided I would do all the things I ever wanted to do before it was too late, so I picked up a guitar and learned how to play. Eventually I started writing my own music, played some backyard shows and even got to play at CSUN for the first annual solfest with a band called Spookydelics. I never would have thought that I would get this far but if you believe anything is possible! I hope I can inspire at least one person to keep reaching for the stars! Much love Louie

Mixchel Payan Pialli! Ni no toca Mixchel. I am 20 years old and I am passionate about music, sounds, and nourishing my barrio. I co-host and DJ a radio show called Mexica Matrix on KQBH LA 101.5FM out of Boyle Heights. On Mexica Matrix, we bring in local musicians and artists to share their art and their stories. As urban natives, our resources to art and ceremony are limited. I'm grateful to explore indigenous stories through a powerful auditory medium that can bring healing to whomever listens. Mexica Matrix broadcasts every Thursday on lpfm.la from 10-11pm.

Bill Ratner is a Northeast Los Angeles Resident and a member of the Emerging Urban Poets. His spoken-word performances are featured on National Public Radio's Good Food, The Business, and KCRW's Strangers. He is a 9-time winner of The Moth Story Slams and 2-time winner of Best of The Hollywood Fringe Extension Award for Solo Performance. He is the voice of "Flint" in the G.I. Joe TV cartoon and "Donnell Udina" in Mass Effect 1, 2 & 3. His work is published in The Chiron Review, The Baltimore Review, Rattle Magazine's Rattlecast, Pleiades, KYSO Flash, South Florida Poetry Journal, The Missouri Review Audio Contest, etc. More info: billratner.com/author

Thelma T. Reyna's books have collectively won 14 national literary awards. She has written six books: a short story collection, *The Heavens Weep for Us and Other Stories*; two poetry chapbooks—*Breath & Bone* and *Hearts in Common*; and three full-length poetry collections—*Rising, Falling, All of Us*; *Reading Tea Leaves After Trump*, which won six national book honors in 2018; and *Dearest Papa: A Memoir in Poems*, (Golden Foothills Press, 2020). As Poet Laureate in Altadena, 2014-2016, she edited the *Altadena Poetry Review Anthology* in 2015 and 2016. Thelma's fiction, poetry, and nonfiction have appeared in literary journals, anthologies, textbooks, blogs, and regional media for over 25 years. She was a Pushcart Prize Nominee in Poetry in 2017. She received her Ph.D. from UCLA..

R.S. Rocha majored in British and American Literature. He received his bachelors in English from California State University, Northridge and was accepted into the Northridge English Master's Program where he continued his literary studies with an emphasis in linguistics, creative writing, and poetry. His major literary influences have been William Faulkner, Ernest Hemingway, Jean-Paul Sartre, Kurt Vonnegut, Jack Kerouac, Patricia Highsmith, Walker Percy, Carlos Fuentes, Gabriel Garcia Márquez, and Thomas Pynchon. Rocha remains indebted to his poetry professor Dr. Benjamin Saltman for teaching him the craft of poetry during his three years of master's studies and Dr. Walter Graves who taught him the fine points of writing prose fiction.

Joshua Rodgers I have been writing all my life as a way to deal with my social anxiety. I always had a lot of feelings and feared to express them so I would wrtie. I am now at a point I want to share my work and inspire others to do the same. If one poem of mine touches one person I will feel overwhelmed with joy for this I believe is my purpose in life.

Susan Rogers, poet, artist and practitioner of Sukyo Mahikari welcomes the blessing of divinity in all things. She considers poetry a vehicle for light and a tool for the exchange of positive energy. She greets her world with an open heart and the spirit of Yokattane, giving a handshake and smile to all those she meets, wishing each soul a seed of something wonderful. Her poetry is included in numerous anthologies and journals including, Altadena Poetry Review, California Quarterly, Kyoto Journal, Saint Julian's Press, San

Diego Poetry Annual: The Best Poems of San Diego, Tiferet. Watch "The Origin is One" at https://www.youtube.com/watch?v=rzPA9zeC0Qc She was interviewed on KPFK by Lois P. Jones and nominated for a Pushcart in 2013 and 2017. Listen to her poetry at: https://www.loispjones.com/susan-rogers/

Michael Romero Retired Education Specialist from L.A.U.S.D., June, 2010. Received B.A. degrees in Art History & Religious Studies, from U.C. Riverside, 1972. Graduated from El Rancho H.S., 1967.

Carla Sameth's memoir, *One Day on the Gold Line* was published on July 2019. Her work appears in literary journals and anthologies including: *Collateral;Brevity Blog*; *Brain, Child*; *Narratively*; *Longreads; MUTHA; Entropy; La Bloga; Tikkun* and *Pasadena Weekly*. Carla was selected to be a Pride Poet with the City of West Hollywood, a PEN In The Community Teaching Artist and has taught creative writing to incarcerated youth through WriteGirl. She teaches at the Los Angeles Writing Project at CSULA and with Southern New Hampshire University. Carla has an MFA in Creative Writing from Queens University. She lives in Pasadena with her wife.

Tony Sandoval is a Xicano poet/professor inspired by the poetry of the master poets of Anahuac and contemporary lyricists within the underground and indigenous music movements.

Sehba Sarwar creates writings and art that tackle displacement, migration, and women's issues. Her work has appeared in *New York Times* Sunday Magazine, *Creative Time Reports*, *Papercuts* and elsewhere. Her short stories have been anthologized by Feminist Press, Akashic Books, and Harper Collins India, while the second edition of her novel, *Black Wings*, was released in 2019. Her papers are archived at the University of Houston's library where she served as artist-in-residence for several years. Born and raised in Karachi Pakistan in a home filled with artists and activists, Sarwar was awarded City of Pasadena's 2019-20 individual artist award.

Elsa M. J. Seifert is an Interfaith Spiritual Director and a long-time resident of Altadena. After raising three sons, managing a business, and editing a Southern California newspaper, she now spends time volunteering for nonprofits and writing essays and poetry. Her poetry has appeared in various anthologies and her prose has appeared in the Southern California Nevada Conference UCC News and in Hometown Pasadena, an online newspaper. She has been writing all her life, found poetry in her soul, and won't stop now.

S. Pearl Sharp Over the past sixty years she has collaborated with other artists merging poetry with dance, music, visual art and film. Published collections include *Typing In The Dark*, the poetry w/jazz CDs *On The Sharp Side* and *Higher Ground* , and 2018 marked the 25th anniversary of her non-fiction *Black Women For Beginners*. A retired documentary filmmaker and former NPR commentator and essayist, she embraces instigating through art. www.spearlsharp.com

Pamela Shea is Sunland-Tujunga's 9th Poet Laureate. She has found poetry to be a wonderful way to chronicle her life, in addition to a means of expression and catharsis. She finds inspiration in family and nature, as well as in triumph and strife. Photography has become a recent artistic passion, and she enjoys combining the two mediums. Pamela has an extensive record of community service. Her professional life includes medical office employment, from which she is retired, and teaching in the fitness field, in which she is still active.

Nancy Shiffrin is the author 3 collections of poems: *Flight, Finishing Line Press, Game With Variations, Wordtech*, and *The Vast Unknowing*, Infinity

Publishing. Her articles and reviews have appeared in the *Los Angeles Times*, *New York Magazine*, *Lummox Journal*, poetix.net and other periodicals.

Dorothy Skiles is a member of the Chupa Rosa Writers, Sunland, 1996-2015. Member of the Village Poets of Sunland-Tununga since 2010. Served as Poet Laureate 2012-2014. Poems appeared in the *Altadena Poetry Review 2016-2019*, (Pushcart Nominee 2017). Poems also appeared in *Meditation on Divine Names*, 2012, *From Benicia With Love*, 2013, and in newspapers and electronic media. Published four chapbooks (two in collaboration). A Member of philanthropic organization that promotes educational opportunities for women.

Beverly A. Tate is an educator with extensive experience at various levels of public teaching. While a teacher in the Los Angeles Unified School District (LAUSD), she was selected as a Mentor and Master teacher. After retiring from Pasadena City College, Beverly created Tate's Consultant Services, LLC (TCS). Her company, TCS, is collaborating with Tia Chucha's Centro Cultural & Bookstore, co-founded by Luis J. and Trini Rodriguez, on a literacy initiative, Black and Latino Men Read.

Mary Langer Thompson Dr. Mary Langer Thompson's articles, short stories, and poetry appear in various journals and anthologies. She is a contributor to *Women and Poetry: Tips on Writing, Teaching and Publishing by Successful Women Poets* (McFarland) and was the 2012 Senior Poet Laureate of California. A retired principal and English teacher, she now writes full time in Apple Valley, California where she received the Jack London Award in 2019 from the High Desert Branch of the California Writers Club

Tim Tipton was first seduced by the craft of poetry when he read the "Panther" by Rainer Marie Rilke. Tim is a graduate of California State University of Northridge where he received a Bachelor of Science in Sociology. He also received a degree in Substance Abuse counseling.

Lauren Tyler-Rickon is a writer and technical-theatre professional; their work explores the intersection of daily life, language, and the natural world we so readily forget we are part of--there is a ringing brightness to the right word in the right place, the right silence at the right time, and the secret glory of light produced by bioluminescent mycellium glowing where there are no eyes to see it, in the vanishing underbelly of forest loam. They live with their loving and supportive spouse not far from Griffith Park and the Glendale Narrows, and love their neighbors: hawks, black-necked stilts, cormorants, and coyotes.

Alexander Uribe's poems talk about his thoughts on the future, the role of media on the perception of people of color, and a hurting relationship.

Amy Uyematsu is a sansei poet and teacher from Los Angeles. She currently leads a writing workshop at the Far East Lounge in downtown Little Tokyo.

Alicia Viguer-Espert, a Mediterranean woman from Spain with roots in the old and the new continent, prefers to keep things light. She loves color, light, and the way people use language to express quotidian and extraordinary experiences. She's been published in *Spectrum, Statement, ZZyZx Writer Z, Lummox, The Altadena Poetry Review* and she's the winner of the San Gabriel Valley Poetry Festival Broadside Contest, and San Gabriel Valley Poetry Festival Book Contest of 2017.

Lori Wall-Holloway is a wife, mother and proud grandmother of nine grandchildren. She lives in the San Gabriel Valley where her poetry has appeared in various publications. More recently, her work has been included in the *Altadena Poetry Review 2015-2019, Spectrum* anthologies, *Lummox 7* and the upcoming *Lummox 8*.

Chris Wallace's homeless career began in 2008. After seven years of living and working on South Avenue 58 in Highland Park, he was evicted from his building. He was the founder of Space Ark Gallery and collective where the small group worked on their music and facilitated other up and coming artivists from the community. Chris was self-taught musician since his early his teens. His art extends to woodcarving and visual art. Through his family's woodcarving and sign business, he was able to afford his first year at Parsons School of Design. After his eviction he started playing music full time. In his imaginative and humorous take on life, music and environment, Chris turns busking into "side walk music" where he decrees from the street, the curb, to the wall is a shared space for everyone, despite what the police, robots and zombies tell him. His sidewalk music is for everybody.

Karen Whitmore I moved to South Pas three years ago and became involved in a Writing Club at the Pasadena Senior Center. I have enjoyed sharing my work with other writers and getting their critiques.

Terry Jean Wilhelm has been writing poetry since the age of ten. Her poems echo the joys and heartaches of living in today's world as a female, as a mother, and as one who loves nature and the earth.

Kath Abela Wilson is creator and leader of Poets on Site in Pasadena, a writing and poetry performance group in homes, gardens,museums and publishing anthologies, active since 2010. She recently edited "*Stone Lantern*" for the Storrier Stearns Japanese Garden, in Pasadena, with James Haddad, owner. Her first book of poetry "*Figures of Humor and Strange Beauty*" was published, 2019, by Glass Lyre Press in Chicago. She is the host and editor of a weekly online Poets Salon on ColoradoBlvd.net for several years, and secretary of Tanka Society of America. She performs her work in concert with her mathematician flute player and collector husband, Rick Wilson, at readings, musical and scientifu=ic conferences worldwide. She sings, dances, and loves yoga and tai chi, plays percussion and tamboura .

Joe Witt In 2015, Joe Witt started Mira Mataric's creative writing class, at the Pasadena Senior Center. There, he learned to love poetry, especially tonkas and haiku. Poetry allows his soul to speak to the universe. He lives in Altadena with his wife, Roz, two cats, Mouse and Shadie Ladie, and our newly acquired rescue dog, Sandy.

C. Jerome Woods, Founding Director of the Black LGBT Project is a published poet and author whose work has appeared in various publications and is recorded on compact disc. He self published *Love Song & Heartbreaks*, a book of poetry, was Managing Editor for International Black Writers & Artists' 3rd anthology, *River Crossings, Voices of the Diaspora* and currently appears in «Jewel›s Catch One» documentary on NetFlix..

The Louisiana native and retired educator sits on several community advisory boards, art panels, and councils. He is a past ACT-SO judge in the Humanities category. In 2009 the National Education Association (NEA) along with the Association for the Study of African Life and History (ASALH) presented him with the Carter G. Woodson Memorial Award "for leadership and creativity in promoting Black History Month, for furthering the understanding of Black Americans' heritage, and for making significant positive changes in a local community."

Although he has been consultant and curator for educational programs and art museums from Lucy Florence Cultural Center in Los Angeles to Las BonFim Jewelers in Salvador da Bahia, Brazil, he is rooted in family, friends, and community. He resides in California where he finds strength, assurance, growth, and tranquility, among his siblings, a host of additional relatives, and an abundance of celebrated others.

Woods hopes to communicate and collaborate with individuals, organizations, agencies, and institutions toward decreasing and/or eradicating HIV/AIDS, homelessness, illiteracy, age and ethnic discrimination, homophobia, incarceration, as well as stigma and shame in the international communi-ty(ies). In addition, while looking at the beauty of his literary, visual, and performance art in promoting good health, healing, and happiness, Woods hopes to produce a major fundraiser, create another book of poetry, and pen a children's book by 2020.

He is community partnering to present an *Archiving 101* workshop for individuals and organizations before the end of this year so that others may be empowered to share their histories, tell their stories, and leave a credible legacy.

Nina Yamamoto I write poetry because it is an inspiring endeavor. I write to give meaning to life's enigmas, and to let quiet moments reveal a sense of fear and wonder. I recently retired and have taken several poetry and other creative writing classes at UCLA Extension. I have been published in the Altadena Poetry Review – 2019, the Haiku Society of America's Members' Anthology, and the Emeritus Chronicles, Spring 2019. I have a B.A. in English from UC Berkeley and an M.A. in English from UCLA.

Sharon Yee I am a Christian Chinese American woman. I was born in California and am an elementary school teacher. I love to draw, paint, and do ceramic sculpture,and write haiku and beginning tanka.I also teach preschool Sunday School and children's ministry. I am on the Mission Committee. I usher at Cerritos Performing Arts Center.

Editorial Board Bios

Khadija Anderson Poet, Mother, Muslim, and Anarchist (not necessarily in that order), Khadija Anderson's poetry has been published extensively online and in print journals and anthologies. Her first book of poetry, "History of Butoh" was published in 2012 by Writ Large Press and a chapbook, "Cul-de-sac: an american childhood" is forthcoming from Ethel Press. Khadija runs a monthly social justice themed poetry series, Poets & Allies for Resistance, in Pasadena.

Carla Sameth As a writer, Carla hopes to help readers feel less alone and more resilient. As a teacher, she strives to help others tell their stories and hone their craft while experimenting with new forms. The journey of motherhood informs much of her writing and she writes about addiction, trauma and resilience with a sense of humor. Carla's memoir, *One Day on the Gold Line*, was published July 2019 by Black Rose. Her essay, "If This Is So, Why Am I" (which is included in her memoir) was listed as a notable in Best American Essays 2019. Her published work can be found at https://carlasameth.com/publications/.

Pauli Dutton I am honored to be on the Editorial Committee for the *Altadena Literary Review 2020*. It is thrilling to have a first look at submissions. The quality, novel modes of expression, and moving words often bring me to tears. Being on the Committee allows me to hang out with wonderful writers, and by listening to their comments, I become better at my craft. I also appreciate the leadership and dedication of Poets Laureate Teresa Mei Chuc and Hazel Clayton Harrison who have made the *Altadena Literary Review 2020* into the new improved *ALR* to include even more forms of writing.

Gerda Govine Ituarte is the Editor of Pasadena Rose Poets Poetry Collection 2019: Reflection. Resistance. Reckoning. Resurrection. Published by Shabda Press with launch on November 15, 2020 at Red Hen Press. She was a panel member during "Career Day in Arts and Culture," at John Muir High School in Pasadena. Her poem, *Temple of Courage Chance Change*, was published in Spectrum 22: Leap Through, in the February 2020 issue which she read at the Pasadena Central Library in February. A speaker series was initiated utilizing her experiences intertwined with poetry during Black History Month at Glendale High School. Govine Ituarte was one of the Selection Committee Members to choose the City of San Diego's first Poet Laureate Ron O. Salisbury. The Pasadena Rose Poets will be highlighting their first poetry collection journey during Pasadena LitFest, May 17-18, 2020, in the Playhouse District.